M000158552

"The cruel military despotism over Burma's Karens has gone on much too long. The West has become inured to it. Benedict Rogers' compassionate story impels readership and compels responses. This is a 'must read' book."   *Bishop David Pytches*

"Lady Mountbatten of Burma once described the Karen people as 'Britain's forgotten allies'. More than anyone I know, Benedict Rogers has made it his business to ensure that the Karen are remembered. *A Land Without Evil* is a first-hand account of their suffering and bravery – written by someone who has regularly put his own life on the line."   *Lord Alton of Liverpool*

"Articulate and powerful . . . *A Land Without Evil* is relevant for anyone interested in facing the dirty truths that often lie beneath the superficiality of international journalism. This is reportage with a conscience . . . a mine of information."
Graham Earnshaw, former Reuters Editor for Asia

"Benedict Rogers knows the truth and makes it compelling and mind-blowing. Once read, this story will never be forgotten."
Dr. Clive Calver, President, World Relief

"Benedict Rogers brings to life one of the most under-reported examples of ethnic repression in modern times. *A Land without Evil* should be read by every responsible citizen of those nations claiming to espouse the principles of global justice."
Dr David Aikman, former senior correspondent of Time *Magazine, and author of* Jesus In Beijing

"For many of us in the Western world evil is long ago and far away. Benedict Rogers' searing account of the atrocities in Burma lifts the lid off our ignorance and leaves us without excuse."
Dr Os Guinness, Senior Fellow, the Trinity Forum

CHRISTIAN SOLIDARITY WORLDWIDE

Christian Solidarity Worldwide is a human rights charity working all over the world on behalf of those who suffer repression. We promote religious liberty for all, with a special focus on the 250 million Christians persecuted for their faith worldwide.

CSW works all over the world . . .

- for *individual prisoners of conscience* like Irene Fernandes awaiting trial in Malaysia for her exposure of human rights abuses, and those *falsely accused* of terrorism in Peru
- for *legislation that adheres to universal standards of religious freedom* such as in Central Asia where registration requirements have denied many their freedom to worship
- for *innocent civilians caught in the crossfire of conflict* such as in Indonesia, Sudan and Nigeria
- for *children in need* such as those in Russia where we operate a pioneering child foster care programme

CSW works to highlight these injustices through raising awareness, campaigning and advocacy. Our publications provide first-hand reports from over 30 countries worldwide, and our supporters are equipped to pray and to write campaign letters to strategic decision makers. Supporters also send cards and letters of encouragement to those in prison. Our staff based in Westminster and Brussels ensure that CSW briefings and urgent appeals reach key officials in the European institutions and foreign ministries as well as the British government. In addition CSW advocacy targets other governments and multi-lateral organisations including the United Nations. Where resources allow, CSW provides humanitarian assistance to those in need.

Proverbs 31:8 "Speak up for those who cannot speak for themselves."

Christian Solidarity Worldwide
PO Box 99
New Malden
Surrey
KT3 3YF

www.csw.org.uk

A Land Without Evil

Stopping the genocide of Burma's Karen people

BENEDICT ROGERS

**MONARCH
BOOKS**

Oxford, UK, & Grand Rapids, Michigan

Copyright © Benedict Rogers 2004.
The right of Benedict Rogers to be identified
as author of this work has been asserted by him in
accordance with the Copyright, Designs
and Patents Act 1988.

All rights reserved.
No part of this publication may be reproduced or
transmitted in any form or by any means, electronic
or mechanical, including photocopy, recording or any
information storage and retrieval system, without
permission in writing from the publisher.

First published in the UK 2004 by Monarch Books
(a publishing imprint of Lion Hudson plc), Mayfield House,
256 Banbury Road, Oxford OX2 7DH.
Tel: +44 (0) 1865 302750 Fax: +44 (0) 1865 302757
Email: monarch@lionhudson.com
www.lionhudson.com

Published in conjunction with
Christian Solidarity Worldwide.

Distributed by:
UK: Marston Book Services Ltd,
PO Box 269, Abingdon, Oxon OX14 4YN;
USA: Kregel Publications, PO Box 2607
Grand Rapids, Michigan 49501.

ISBN 1 85424 646 1 (UK)
ISBN 0 8254 6059 X (USA)

Cover photo: Brian McCartan

Unless otherwise stated, Scripture quotations are
taken from the Holy Bible, New International Version,
© 1973, 1978, 1984 by the International Bible Society.
Used by permission of Hodder and Stoughton Ltd.
All rights reserved.

British Library Cataloguing Data
A catalogue record for this book is available
from the British Library.

Book design and production for the publishers by
Bookprint Creative Services
P.O. Box 827, BN21 3YJ, England.
Printed in Great Britain.

For my Karen friends and all who are engaged in the struggle for democracy, freedom and justice in Burma, and for all the peoples of Burma, that they may be able to know and fulfil the meaning of unity in diversity

"The body is a unit, though it is made up of many parts; and though all its parts are many, they form one body. So it is with Christ."
1 Corinthians 12:12

CONTENTS

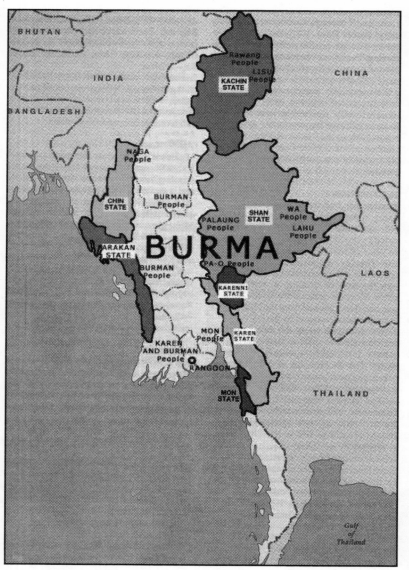

AN IMPASSIONED PLEA FROM A KAREN PASTOR

Kawthoolei, which literally means "a land without blemish", has long been a land with mines and a killing field. Burma, once the "rice bowl of Asia", is now one of the Least Developed Countries in the world. Fifty-four years of fighting a civil war, more than forty years under the military dictatorship, and for many of us living more than one and a half decades in exile as illegal immigrants or displaced people is long enough!

On behalf of our Karen people and all the ethnic groups of Burma, we would like to request both the military regime and all the parties concerned to stop fighting and find a peaceful solution to the long-existing problem. The only way to have lasting peace is through having mutual love, understanding, forgiveness, recognition, negotiation and reconciliation.

We would also like to humbly and earnestly request all the international community to be willing to serve as "peacemakers" and help us. We are tired of hearing news of both the soldiers and civilians – Burmans, Chin, Kachin, Karen, Mon, Arakan and Shan – our own people, brothers and sisters coexisting and living together in the same country – being injured, tortured or killed in the battles. Our hearts are saturated with hearing news of fighting, human rights abuses and atrocities committed without discrimination of age, sex, race and religion. Please help stop the civil war in Burma and help restore peace and stability to Burma. It will be good, not only for us, but also for all.

We are badly in need of your immediate response, action and kind help. Help us through any ways and means you can. Most of all we need your prayer support that God will intervene and change the situation in Burma for His own glory and honour. Thank you all so much for helping us throughout the years and for your continuous help and support. May God bless you all as you continue to serve Him through helping your needy brothers and sisters.

Reverend Simon
Secretary of the Kawthoolei Karen Baptist Convention
Principal of the Kawthoolei Karen Baptist Convention
Bible School and College

ABOUT THE AUTHOR

Benedict Rogers is a freelance journalist and human rights campaigner. He has worked with the international Christian human rights organisation, Christian Solidarity Worldwide (CSW), since 1994. He founded CSW UK's youth section, served as a member of the Board of Management of CSW UK, founded CSW Hong Kong, and worked in Washington DC as a consultant to CSW. He currently serves as CSW's Advocacy Officer for South Asia. He is also a trustee of the Metta Trust for Children's Education.

Ben has visited the Karen people on both sides of the Thai–Burmese border six times since 2000. He has also worked with the Karenni, Shan and Chin ethnic nationalities. He has contributed articles on Burma to *The Asian Wall Street Journal*, *The Sunday Times*, *The Irrawaddy*, *The Catholic Herald*, *Crisis* and *Christianity Today*, and has also written for *The Daily Telegraph*, *The Times*, *The Tablet*, *The Hong Kong Standard* and other publications. He has appeared regularly on radio in the UK, USA and Hong Kong, and is a regular speaker at conferences and in churches around the world.

From 1997 until 2002, Ben worked as a journalist in Hong Kong. He has also worked in East Timor and China.

He has an MA in China Studies from the School of Oriental and African Studies, and wrote his dissertation on the Chinese Government's attitude towards Christianity. He is also the co-author of *The Life & Death of a Dotcom in China*.

ABBREVIATIONS

ABSDF	All Burma Students Democratic Front
AFPFL	Anti-Fascist People's Freedom League
BSPP	Burmese Socialist Programme Party
DAB	Democratic Alliance of Burma
DKBA	Democratic Karen Buddhist Army
KNLA	Karen National Liberation Army
KNU	Karen National Union
NCUB	National Coalition of the Union of Burma
NCGUB	National Coalition Government of the Union of Burma
NDF	National Democratic Front
NLD	National League for Democracy
SPDC	State Peace and Development Council
SSA	Shan State Army

The following Burmese and Karen terms are used widely throughout the book:

Saw is roughly equivalent to "Mr"
Daw is "Mrs"
Naw is "Miss"
Padoh signifies a leader among the Karen

ACKNOWLEDGEMENTS

While I have drawn for background purposes on the works of other authors, notably Martin Smith, Shelby Tucker, Donald Mackenzie Smeaton, Don Richardson and Christian Goodden, whose works are referenced in the endnotes at the end of each chapter and in the bibliography, the primary sources of information and material for this book have been people whom I have interviewed personally. In the endnotes, I have only referenced material from other publications – where information, or a quotation, is without a reference, it is from one of these personal interviews.

On the Thai–Burmese border, I was privileged to have the opportunity to interview the President of the Karen National Union (KNU), Padoh Ba Thin Sein; the Vice-President and Minister of Defence, General Bo Mya; General Shwe Hser; the General Secretary, Padoh Mahn Sha; the Joint General Secretary Htoo Htoo Lay; Hla Henry, a member of the Committee for Internally Displaced Karen People (CIDKP); Colonel Nerdah Mya, commander of Battalion 201 and a spokesman on foreign affairs; Colonel Soe Soe; Pastor Winai; Reverend Dr Simon; Major Mary On; Lydia Tamlawah; Saw Tamlawah; Micah Rollings; Dr Cynthia Maung; Doh Say;

Ner Soe, and many other Karen. I also met with Min Zaw Oo, a Burman democracy activist in Chiang Mai. To them I express my gratitude for their time and willingness to share experiences, stories and opinions. I am also grateful to Zing Cung, General Secretary of the National Democratic Front (NDF); Kho Than Khe, Chairman of the All Burma Students Democratic Front (ABSDF); Dr Thein Lwin of Teacher Training for Burmese Teachers; Edythe McCarty of the Thailand Baptist Missionary Fellowship; Jack Dunford of the Burmese Border Consortium; Tha-U-Wah-A-Pah and the Free Burma Rangers; and other friends in the Burmese democracy movement and foreign missionary and non-governmental organisations.

In the United States, I would like to record my appreciation of the help, advice and information given to me by Louisa Benson Craig, Naw May Oo, Show Ei Tun, Robert Zan, Stephen Dun, Laurie Dawson, Lian Uk, Moe Thee Zun, Aung Din, Aung Saw Oo, Roland Maung, Bawi Lian Maung and the Prime Minister of the National Coalition Government of the Union of Burma, Dr Sein Win. I would also like to pay tribute to the excellent work of the Free Burma Coalition and the US Campaign for Burma, and my friends Jeremy Woodrum and Dan Beaton. In the US Congress, the commitment of Senator Mitch McConnell, Senator Sam Brownback and Congressman Joseph Pitts, and their staff, is of tremendous value to the struggle for freedom in Burma.

In the United Kingdom, I met with former political prisoner Ko Aung; KNU Representative in Germany, Maung Kyaw; KNU Representative in Europe, Saw Sarky; Euro-Burma Director Harn Yawnghwe; former British soldiers Major Ian Abbey and Colonel Michael Osborn; and I corresponded with another former soldier, Captain Tony Bennett. Major Abbey and Captain Bennett provided me with a variety of documents, including personal correspondence, which have not until now been published, and so I am deeply grateful to them for their help. I also corresponded with Thelma Gyi-Baerlein, daughter of Saw Ba U Gyi, and with Paul Stzumpf, his grandson, and I appreciate the materials they kindly provided.

Several friends helped by proof-reading and fact-checking prior to publication, and these included: Sarah Weyler, Kelsey Hoppe, James Mawdsley, Hamilton Walters and Todd Deatherage. I appreciate their help, and wise counsel. Furthermore, I thank Tony Collins and all the team at Monarch for their guidance and hard work.

Lastly, I would like to thank my friends and colleagues who are also engaged and committed to the cause of human rights and democracy in Burma, particularly Lord Alton and James Mawdsley, and my friends in Christian Solidarity Worldwide, Baroness Cox, Dr Martin Panter, Lydia Haines, Lyla Stephens and Anthony Peel. Their inspiration, encouragement, friendship and assistance with this book have been invaluable.

FOREWORD

By the Baroness Cox of Queensbury

This morning dawned cloudy in the borderlands between Thailand and Burma. But as the sun breaks through, the beauty is breathtaking: high, rugged mountains; thick green jungle; rich fertile valleys surrounding free-flowing rivers.

The beauty is so exhilarating it nearly makes us forget why we are here. It seems almost impossible to believe this apparent paradise is a place more like hell for hundreds of thousands of people around us. The conflict of emotions caused by the contrast between the beauty of the land and the enormity of the tragedy of the oppressed and displaced people nearby is made even more acute by another bittersweet contrast – the brutality of a regime which inflicts immeasurable suffering on countless innocent people and the responses of its victims: dignity in deprivation; generosity in destitution and a love which transforms brutality into miracles of grace.

As I write this foreword, I am returning from another visit to the Karen and Karenni people in exile in Thailand and across the border in their traditional homeland in Burma. During the past few days, I have been privileged to visit many of the contemporary heroes and heroines described so eloquently in this book. I have also met many more victims of the ethnic cleansing being perpetrated by the Burmese ruling junta with its Orwellian name: the State Peace and Development Council (SPDC). I can therefore testify to the accuracy and authenticity of Benedict Rogers' moving accounts of the plight of the ethnic groups such as the Karen, Karenni and Shan in Burma today and endorse the poignant appropriateness of the title he has chosen for this book. For the people I have met during many visits are truly innocent victims of a regime which is inflicting all manner of evils upon them: military offensives against civilians; enforced labour as porters for the Burmese army in conditions so harsh that many perish – especially the elderly who have to carry 30 kgs of ammunition for the soldiers for days on end, without adequate rest, food or water; the use of civilians as human minesweepers; and a multiplicity of atrocities inflicted on unarmed villagers, including systematic torture, rape and killing.

But those whom I have met during many visits over the past ten years consistently refuse to match evil with evil. Instead, they endure their suffering with dignity and without hatred. For example, we support two homes for Karen and Karenni children who have lost parents as a result of the SPDC's brutal policies. Some have seen their fathers and mothers slaughtered. But yesterday, they sang songs of hope with no hint of bitterness and the inevitable traces of suffering in their faces were tempered by smiles of genuine joy and love.

This spirit is also illustrated by the Reverend Dr Simon, a Karen pastor who has turned the limitations of exile in a camp for the displaced into a home for children in need, a school and a theological college. A few days ago, he gave me a recent meditation which he composed, based on some words from a well-known Christmas carol:

> I wonder as I wander
> On life's journey as a refugee,

Away from home and loved ones,
About all the news I have heard and seen,
Full of untold miseries:
People killed and being killed,
People raped and being raped;
People oppressed and being oppressed,
People sold and being sold;
People held and being held,
Detained in many ways
Imprisoned, jailed and house arrest . . .
But then I wonder as I wander,
A child of God on life's journey . . .
About unfolding mysteries:
People loved and being loved;
People helped and being helped;
Kind people showing kindness,
Following the Master's steps,
Fulfilling His holy word . . .

Benedict Rogers' book vividly portrays the poignancy of the plight of the ethnic national peoples of Burma, focusing primarily on the Karen people. Hundreds of thousands have fled from their homelands in order to survive. They are living inevitably stunted lives in the privations of the camps strung along the Thai border with Burma. Countless more are living as displaced people within Burma, hiding in the jungle, living in constant terror of being found and killed by SPDC troops. They have no proper shelter; no access to medical care; no education, other than the occasional rudimentary primary school. Three days ago I met a young mother still living inside Burma who had watched helplessly as three of her five children died of malaria. On a previous visit, I talked to a young man who had been forced to work as a porter for Burmese soldiers and to act as a human minesweeper. He trod on a mine which severed one leg and badly burnt the other. The soldiers left him to die in the jungle. When word of his fate got back to his village, his uncle came to rescue him, but on the way his uncle was killed by a mine. Eventually, after two days, the young man was rescued just in time to save his life. He was recovering, but there was no way he could obtain a prosthesis.

This book also puts the current situation into a historical context, which helps the reader to understand many of the complex and conflicting issues which shape the current political situation. It describes the long-standing oppression by Burmese rulers of the ethnic national groups such as the Karen, Karenni, Mon, Shan, Chin and Arakan. It also gives detailed accounts of numerous ways in which these peoples, especially the Karen, supported the British in diverse military campaigns. The most famous examples date from the Second World War, when many Karen gave their lives fighting alongside British troops and many others endured torture and death in order to protect British soldiers. Consequently, during the post-war negotiations for a political settlement, they looked to the British for support in their passionate quest for an independence which would enable them to live safely in their own lands. But the British sided with the Burmese and forced the ethnic national groups into a political union in which they were inherently vulnerable. Subsequent decades of oppression and resistance have ensued. The suffering we witness today is a manifestation of the tragic outcomes of those decisions, which are seen by the Karen and others as a betrayal by the British. However, they still hope that we who are British will remember the debts we owe. They also hope that the international community will support them as they try to defend their fundamental human rights to basic freedoms – including the freedom to live in peace in their own lands. I therefore hope that this book will challenge those of us who have the privilege of living in freedom to use our freedoms to speak and work for those who are denied them.

Although this book is a challenge, it is not ultimately depressing. For its catalogue of suffering and perceived betrayal is redeemed by many characters who inspire the reader with stories of "amazing grace". Visitors to these lands can meet many of them today. I have met some this week and I return to Britain humbled and inspired. Written from an explicitly Christian perspective, the book speaks for all who suffer, whether Christian, Buddhist, Muslim or Animist. It portrays human qualities of courage and dignity of people of diverse faiths and cultures whose lives shine as beacons of light in a very dark part of the world. It is their voices which speak through the pages of this book, yearning for their freedom. Are we going to listen and to respond? Or are we going to let their pleas for justice fall on deaf ears – again?

Caroline Cox
Deputy Speaker of the House of Lords
Honorary President, Christian Solidarity Worldwide – UK
22nd November 2003

INTRODUCTION

In early 2001, three Karen men, Maw Ti Ae, Maw Ae and Pa La Sae, were minding their own business in their village, when the Burma Army arrived. Accusing them of supporting the Karen resistance, the soldiers shot the men on the spot. The three were buried at the entrance to the village, with their heads above ground. The villagers were warned to leave them like that, as a warning to others. They were told that if they touched the bodies, they would suffer the same fate.

The title of this book, *A Land Without Evil*, is both a paradoxical and an aspirational title.

It is paradoxical because Burma today, and Karen State in particular, is a land torn apart by evil. It is a land ruled by a regime which took power by force, ignored the will of the people in an election, and survives by creating a climate of fear. It is a land terrorised by a military regime which to this day perpetrates a catalogue of crimes against humanity. It takes people for forced labour, uses villagers as human minesweepers, captures children and forces them to become soldiers, systematically rapes ethnic minority women, and burns down villages and crops. It is a regime which has killed thousands of people in the ethnic minority areas, particularly the

Karen, Karenni and Shan, and has slaughtered thousands of Burman students. Over a million people are now displaced in the jungles of eastern Burma, perhaps as many as two million in the entire country, and there are hundreds of thousands of refugees across the border in Thailand, India and Bangladesh. All this is part of a concerted effort known as the "Four Cuts", introduced by the regime in the 1970s: to cut off from the resistance forces supplies of food, funds, intelligence and recruits. The strategy is to undermine the armed resistance by terrorising the civilian population and destroying their livelihoods.

Politicians would call these acts "human rights violations", but theologically and morally, the word "evil" is more appropriate. In March 1990, for example, the Commanding Officer of the Burma Army's 8th Regiment, Soe Win, seized cattle from Karen villagers worth 350,000 kyats and pigs worth 50,000 kyats. His men then shot and killed a 50-year-old woman at Thay-kay-ti village, and then murdered her 16-year-old son. They then tore out his liver and heart and ate them.[1] If that is not evil, what is? In another incident, a fifteen-year-old Karen girl was walking with her father. A Burma Army soldier appeared, shot the father dead, and then raped the girl. After raping her, he then put the barrel of his gun into the girl's vagina and shot her dead. "This is not an ordinary crime, this is a dirty crime," said the man who told me that story. If that is not evil, what is?

In addition to murdering and torturing thousands of people, the Burmese junta, known as the State Peace and Development Council (SPDC), is a regime deeply involved in the drugs trade, making Burma the world's largest opium producer. According to Christian Goodden, in his book *Three Pagodas*, the infamous "Golden Triangle", of which Burma is a part, produces 2,000 tons of opium a year, the equivalent of 200 tons of pure heroin, and millions of amphetamine pills.[2]

It has been claimed that 80 per cent of Australia's drugs, and perhaps as much as 60 per cent of the heroin in the United States, originated in Burma.[3] It is estimated that a billion methamphetamine pills were sold by Burma in 2002 alone,[4] and between 900 million and one billion methamphetamine tablets, worth £2 billion, will be exported across the Thai border in 2004.[5] While for some years the junta and Khun Sa, the world's best known drug baron, were in conflict, in 1996 they struck a deal. Khun Sa effectively handed over his lucrative drugs trade, his personal army, and his alliance with the United Wa State Army (UWSA), to the SPDC in exchange for a peaceful retirement in a mansion in Rangoon, protected from extradition to the United States where he would face criminal charges. Now, the regime uses the UWSA, "one of the world's great drug cartels" led by Pao U Chang, and in particular the UWSA's southern brigade commander, "the area's most powerful warlord" Wei Siao-gang,[6] to fight the Shan resistance forces. The junta also reached a truce with the warlord Lo Hsing-han in 1987, and now, according to the Shan resistance leader Colonel Yawd Serk, he is "a successful business partner of the Burmese generals".

Meanwhile, the Karen have adopted a strict anti-drugs policy and have destroyed several methamphetamine factories along the Thai–Burmese border. "We forbid the growth, sale and use of drugs," the former President of the Karen National Union (KNU), General Bo Mya told me. "We take very strong action against anyone involved. We are doing this to protect humanity." People caught taking, possessing or dealing in drugs face severe penalties and have been known to be executed by the Karen. But the Karen receive no international assistance in their war on drugs.

Burma is also a land facing a crisis of HIV/AIDS. And it is a country whose economy has been wrecked by the government. It has sunk from being one of the wealthiest nations in the region, the "rice basket" of Asia, to ranking now as one of the world's ten poorest nations. In December 1987 Burma sought and obtained Least Developed Country status. Despite this, the junta spends only 0.5 per cent of its GDP on education and health,[7] while spending almost 50 per cent on the military. It has expanded its armed forces to approaching 500,000 troops, and General Than Shwe, the head of state, has been ranked number five in a list of the world's *10 Worst Living Dictators*.[8]

It is a land of religious persecution. In 2001, 50 churches in Rangoon, the capital, were closed down and the regime built their biggest ever Buddhist pagoda. It has been ranked as one of the six worst violators of religious freedom by the US State Department. It is, sadly, a land full of evil.

But the title of this book is also aspirational, because the people of Burma want peace, freedom and justice, and they have been struggling for these ever since independence. The Karen people have been fighting the longest, and have sacrificed and suffered the most. It is their hope, and mine, that one day their country will truly be a land without evil.

A Land Without Evil is also one translation of the name for the Karen people's land, Kawthoolei. There are other possible translations for Kawthoolei – "Land of Light", "Land of the Black Flower", "Garden of Flowers" – but "Land Without Evil" conveys best the gap between hope and reality. In the Karen National Union (KNU)'s pamphlet entitled *The Karens and their Struggle for Freedom*, the name is explained:

The Karens named this land Kaw-Lah, meaning the Green Land. We began to peacefully clear and till our land free from all hindrance. Our labours were fruitful and we were very happy with our lot. So we changed the name of the land to Kawthoolei, a land free of all evils, famine, misery and strife: Kawthoolei, a pleasant, plentiful and peaceful country. Here we lived characteristically simple, uneventful and peaceful lives, until the advent of the Burman.[9]

This is a book about the Karen people and their struggle, but it is also intended to reflect the wider struggle that all the people of Burma are fighting. The other ethnic nationalities, such as the Chin, Kachin, Shan, Karenni, Arakan and Mon, are also engaged in the fight for freedom and have suffered similar atrocities. And the majority Burmans themselves, led by Nobel Laureate Daw Aung San Suu Kyi, have given much to their campaign for democracy. Daw Aung San Suu Kyi herself personified the struggle, with her own sacrifice of personal freedom for the sake of the wider cause. When she walked, smiling, towards a row of soldiers pointing guns directly at her in 1989, symbolising non-violent defiance, she won the hearts of all who care about justice. She has also identified with the Karen, saying: "The sufferings of our Karen brothers and sisters are our very own sufferings."[10]

Burma has a population of almost 50 million, with over 100 different languages spoken. It is, as Paul Sztumpf, grandson of the first Karen resistance leader Saw Ba U Gyi, said, "a tapestry of nations, religions and cultures". The official name of the country was changed by the SPDC to "Myanmar", but I shall continue to use the name "Burma" in this book. Those who care about democracy and freedom in Burma prefer to use that name, because it was an illegitimate government which changed the name of the country, without any mandate from the people to do so. Daw Aung San Suu Kyi, and the Karen too, have expressed their desire for us to continue to call it Burma, in defiance of the SPDC.

It is important at this stage to note two points of style in this book. The terms "Burman" and "Burmese" are often used interchangeably by people, but they actually have specific meanings. "Burman" refers to the ethnic group which is the majority in Burma; "Burmese" refers to all citizens of Burma. I shall use these terms as they are intended to be used, although in direct quotations I have used the terms as spoken by the source. Furthermore, some writers use the word "Burmese" loosely, referring to the regime or its military. But that gives the impression that the entire Burmese population is attacking the ethnic minorities, and that is far from true. So when referring to the regime or its military, I shall do so specifically, to distinguish it from the Burman or Burmese people. I shall use the terms "SPDC", "junta" or "regime"; and when referring to the military, I shall use either "the Burma Army" or its Burmese name, the "Tatmadaw".

The Karen, along with the Shan, are the largest ethnic nationality in Burma besides the majority Burmans. They dislike the term "ethnic minority" because they make up a substantial portion of the population. Indeed, along with the other non-Burman ethnic nationalities, they make up 40 per cent of the population and inhabit 60 per cent of the land. They are also some of the earliest inhabitants of what is now Burma.

In the Second World War the Japanese put the Karens at 4.5 million. Some Karens now claim their population amounts to 10 or 12 million, but these figures sound wildly inflated. The KNU itself claims 7 million, although even this may be optimistic.[11] The SPDC claims 2.5 million Karens, and this is likely to be an underestimate. A realistic conservative estimate by Operation World puts the Karen population in Burma at around 4.8 million. However, no accurate census has been carried out so real figures are impossible to find.

Whatever the true figure, however, they have more people than many small independent nations. They also have all the characteristics of a nation: a government structure, albeit largely in exile in Thailand; a language, a history, an army and a flag. They are also more than one ethnic nationality – within the Karen "ethnic group" are at least 20 sub-groups. These include the two principal branches of the Karen, the Sgaw and Pwo, but also other groups which are fighting their own struggles for autonomy and self-determination: the Karenni or "Red Karen", the Pa-O and the Padaung, for example. But "the Karen" as a whole have been fighting for their survival for well over half a century. The Karens' armed struggle ranks as one of the longest-running civil wars in history.

While the origins of this civil war undoubtedly had racial and cultural tones to it, and the Karens had suffered much at the hands of the Burmans for centuries, it became a political struggle for freedom and self-determination after the Second World War, and in the past few decades it has become a struggle specifically against a brutal oppressive regime in Burma. For that reason, while there are issues to be resolved between the Karens and the Burmans, it is important to focus on what they have in common in the current struggle. There is distrust between the Karens and the Burmans, but through this struggle against the SPDC some barriers have been broken down. The Karens, along with the Shan, Karenni, Chin, Kachin, Arakan, Mon and other ethnic groups, share a common cause with the Burman democracy movement. And the Karen are no longer officially fighting for independence, a cause for which they still yearn in their hearts but which they know is unrealistic, even though there are elements who still see it as their ultimate goal. Instead, they call for "tripartite dialogue" between the SPDC, the Burman democracy movement and the ethnic groups, resulting in a permanent ceasefire and a federal political structure for Burma in which the Karen and the other ethnic states will have significant autonomy and equal rights.

The Karens are often perceived as a "Christian" tribe, and their legends, described in Chapter One, have extraordinary parallels with the Old Testament. Many Karens have inspiring Christian faith, and much of the Karen leadership is

Christian. However, it is a mistake to portray them entirely as a Christian tribe, as it is estimated that only 40 per cent are Christian, while the majority of the people are Buddhist or Animist.

But the Christians among the Karen have suffered the most intense persecution. They are targeted more than others by the SPDC. When Burma Army soldiers attack a Karen village, they often ask villagers what their religion is. In an attack on Huay Kaloke refugee camp, on the Thai side of the border, in 1998, the Baptist church was among the first buildings to be torched. The Buddhist monastery and the homes around it were left untouched.[12]

However, while this book is written from a Christian perspective, it is important to remember that this is not primarily a religious war, it is a political war in which religion is used as a tool of oppression. While the regime in Burma uses Buddhism and Buddhists as a political tool to oppress other religions, notably the Christian Karen, Karenni, Chin and Kachin, when it suits them, the majority of Buddhists in the country are not only peaceful but are also supportive of the struggle for justice and are suffering under the tyranny of this regime. The Buddhist Shans and the Muslim Rohingya are persecuted too. As the former Karen President General Bo Mya said, "this is not a war between the Christians and Buddhists, it is between the Burm[ans] and the Karen. But they are using religion as a tool to divide people. They hate everybody, not just Christians. They're not only killing Christians. They're killing Buddhists as well. But they are especially targeting Christians."[13]

I would therefore wish to emphasise that while I describe incidents where Christians have been attacked by "Buddhist" soldiers, it is the crimes themselves which I and the Karen people hate, not the Buddhist people. Jesus taught us to love our neighbours as ourselves, and to hate the sin, but to love the sinner. Therefore, while this book is unashamedly Christian in tone, it is not anti-Buddhist. I wish to pay tribute to the many Buddhists in Burma who are engaged in the struggle for justice, and especially to acknowledge the profound inspiration and example which Daw Aung San Suu Kyi provides.

But there is a spiritual battle at the heart of this struggle, the battle between right and wrong, good and evil. The type of oppression that takes place is not merely political – restrictions on freedom of speech, association and religion. The acts are violent and vulgar, even depraved. They are acts carried out by a regime that has no knowledge of or regard for God, or even for goodness, but instead only worships power and is determined to cling onto it by all means. They are acts of genocide.

There is an even deeper spiritual undertone to this conflict. Ne Win, who led the coup in 1962 and founded the Burmese Socialist Programme Party (BSPP) and the ideology known as "The Burmese Way to Socialism", was an extremely superstitious man. He developed an involvement in black magic and the occult, and in astrology, which led to some eccentric, and devastating, policies. He was told that the number nine was his lucky number, so he demonetised banknotes that were not divisible by nine, and instead issued notes of strange denominations, such as 45 and 90. Overnight, ordinary citizens lost years of savings.

Ne Win appeared puritanical – he banned ballroom dancing and horse racing, and had expressed conservative views about women – yet he was married seven times and was a devoted gambler. It is said that he banned horse racing after a bookie at Ascot cheated him. In 1984 the *Far Eastern Economic Review* reported that a privately chartered jet taking Ne Win to a Swiss health clinic "was delayed because chests of jade and precious stones carried on board had been stacked incorrectly and had to be reloaded" – three years later, Burma applied for Least Developed Nation status to seek foreign debt relief.

Harn Yawnghwe, a committed Christian and son of the first President of Burma, Sao Shwe Thaike, told a meeting in London on the Global Day of Prayer for Burma that Ne Win's rule led to a "spiritual darkness" in Burma. "We need the power of God to break that," he said.

While this book is about the Karen, and it is a tribute to their courage amidst such suffering, it is not a eulogy to them. Some people, particularly former British soldiers who served alongside Karens in the Second World War, view the Karen with rose-tinted spectacles. Yet while many Karen are exceptionally gracious, gentle, hospitable, generous, courageous and faithful, they are human beings. And like all human beings, they fall short. They are not perfect. They are simply people, doing their best to fight for justice, to hold on to their homeland, to seek the basic right to self-determination, and to uphold their faith in God. They do this with great grace, and I have nothing but deep admiration, respect and affection for them, but I also know that they have, as all people do, made mistakes. They have too often allowed divisions to emerge within their groups which have held back their cause. One foreign missionary working among the Karen told me that acts of evil have been committed by Karen against Karen. This book has not attempted to hide that fact, although the balance of injustice, depravity and cruelty undoubtedly rests with the junta.

I have visited the Thai–Burmese border six times. I have spent time with Karen and Karenni refugees in the camps in Thailand, but I have also crossed into Burma on several occasions, to visit the internally displaced people in Karen and Shan States. I have crossed the Moei river, trekked through the jungle, slept in bamboo huts among the resistance soldiers, and bought supplies of medicine, rice, coffee, candles and waterproof jackets for Karen troops. Each time I cross into Burma I do so illegally, with the resistance. But in my view, it is not me who is illegal, it is the SPDC. In 1990 it held elections, which were overwhelmingly won by the National League for Democracy, yet the SPDC clings to power. It is an illegitimate regime. So because I do not believe that this regime's laws are God's laws, and I believe that God calls us to reach out to the persecuted and suffering regardless of borders, I have no hesitation making that crossing. I do it without passport or visa – the Holy Spirit is my visa.

Some people might accuse me of being biased, and they would be correct. But I am biased not so much in favour of the Karen, although many of them have become my friends, but more in favour of justice, freedom and democracy. I am biased against injustice and brutality. And for that reason I have written this book not so much as a historical, or anthropological scholarly work, but as a call to action. For too long the people of Burma, especially the Karen, have suffered, and for too long the world has sat idly by. It is time that ordinary people, ordinary Christians, in the free world – Britain, the rest of Europe, the United States, Australia, Canada – took to the streets in the way they did against apartheid in South Africa. It is time people rose up and appealed loudly to our governments to take action to end the genocide in Burma. It is often said by Christians that the collapse of the Iron Curtain and the Soviet Empire came about through many years of prayer. It is time, then, that people prayed for Burma – every day.

Thomas à Kempis, in his book *The Imitation of Christ*, argues that "those who love stay awake when duty calls, wake up from sleep when someone needs help; those who love keep burning, no matter what, like a lighted torch". Such people "take on anything, complete goals, bring plans to fruition". But those who do not love "faint and lie down on the job".

Those of us in the free world have a responsibility to speak for those who cannot speak for themselves. We cannot afford to faint and lie down on the job. The words of William Wilberforce, when introducing legislation to end the slave trade, should ring in our ears as we consider the stories of persecution in our modern day world: "We can no longer plead ignorance. We cannot turn aside." I believe God has called us to stay awake – individually and corporately, practically and spiritually – until the day when justice is done and freedom comes to Burma. He calls us to keep burning like a lighted torch.

Benedict Rogers

NOTES

1 Karen National Union, *Human Rights Atrocities by the Burma Army 8th Regiment*, March 31st, 1990
2 Christian Goodden, *Three Pagodas: A Journey Down the Thai–Burmese Border*, p. 81
3 Timothy Laklem, *Burma: The Facts*
4 Congressman Joseph Pitts, H. Res 84, House of Representatives, 108th Congress, February 13th, 2003
5 Lord Astor of Hever, House of Lords debate on Burma, *Hansard*, December 3rd, 2002
6 Goodden, p. 151
7 Lord Chan, Debate on Burma, House of Lords, June 24th, 2003
8 *Parade Magazine*, February 16, 2003
9 KNU, *The Karens and their Struggle for Freedom*, November 2000, p. 5
10 Quoted by Lord Alton, House of Lords debate on Burma and Karen Refugees, *Hansard*, March 25th, 1998
11 Martin Smith, *Burma: Insurgency and the Politics of Ethnicity*, p. 30

12 Mark O'Keefe, "Government soldiers seize on faith as a tactic to terrorize and divide the region's refugees", October 28th, 1998, *The Oregonian*
13 Ibid.

CHAPTER ONE

THE GOLDEN BOOK

"For it is one thing to see the land of peace from a wooded
ridge . . .
. . . and another to tread the road that leads to it"
St Augustine, *Confessions*

As the little boat neared the shore on the Burmese side of the Moei river, I saw the reality of the decades-long Karen struggle for the first time. Just a few weeks previously, under the trees by the river, opposite Thailand, had stood a thriving Karen village. There was a school, a clinic, houses and a church. Now, almost all that was left were the ashes.

The Burma Army, known as the Tatmadaw, accompanied by their militia, the Democratic Karen Buddhist Army (DKBA),[1] had attacked this village. It was not the first time, and it was unlikely to have been the last. The villagers had been on the move for years, fleeing one attack and building new settlements upriver every year or so. Mercifully, in this particular attack the people received prior warning from Karen National Liberation Army (KNLA) scouts on lookout. They escaped across the border to Thailand. But the Karen are not always so fortunate.

I stood amidst the ruins of the church, a few pews still standing within the charred frame of the bamboo building. A

cross hung limply at the front. It may not even have originally
been a cross. It was more likely the remains of one of the
beams that had once held up the roof. But now it was a cross,
and it symbolised the people's suffering.

As I stood there, the words uttered by a senior Burmese
general a few years before echoed in my mind. In a public statement in 1992, Major-General Ket Sein, the South East Regional
Commander who was then promoted to Health Minister in the
ruling junta ironically known as the State Peace and Development Council (SPDC), proclaimed the regime's intention that
"in ten years all Karen will be dead. If you want to see a Karen,
you will have to go to a museum in Rangoon". The sickening
image of General Maung Aye, the SPDC's deputy chairman,
stamping on a Karen flag and forcing a Karen leader to kneel
before him and apologise for their rebellion, shown on
Myanmar TV in February 1996, also came to mind.

I sat on one of the pews. I had to be careful where I walked,
as the surrounding area was full of landmines. I imagined
what this burned-out bamboo church building had been like
just a few weeks before. Filled with the sound of beautiful
singing, the Karens would have been dressed in their traditional red tunics and sarongs or *longyis*. The words of hymns
such as "Amazing Grace" would have been juxtaposed with
"Onward Christian Soldiers". On the wall above the platform
where the pastor and elders sat would have been words of
Scripture, probably the words that were now on display in the
newly built church upriver: "Be thou faithful unto death and
I will give thee a crown of life", from Revelation 2:10.

The pastor arrived and surveyed the wreckage. He looked
into my eyes and with sadness mixed with faith, he said: "We
have to leave village after village, house after house. But it
increases our faith. We are Christians. We know God will help
us. But please remember us in your prayers. Please do not
forget."

The history of the Karen people, the largest ethnic nationality in Burma besides the majority Burmans, has been inter-
woven with the Gospel for centuries – even before the first
missionaries reached the area. Although the majority of
Karens are still either Buddhist or Animist, they are often considered a "Christian" tribe. Most of the leadership of the
Karen resistance is Christian. Some people even suggest they
are one of the lost tribes of Israel. This is largely due to the
Karens' own traditional legends.

For centuries, the Karen believed that they had once possessed a "Golden Book" which contained the truth about life.
This book had been taken by a younger white brother across
the seas. One day, the young white brother would return with
the book.

In 1795 a British diplomat from the embassy in Rangoon
visited a Karen village, accompanied by a Burman guide.
Immediately the villagers surrounded him and greeted him
with delight, believing he was the white man returning their
book. But the Burman guide became anxious when the Karen
villagers started telling the diplomat that they believed that the
white man, having given them the lost book, would set them
free from all their oppressors. The diplomat was there to arbitrate a dispute between Britain and Burma, which Burma
feared might cause Britain to invade, and he sensed his guide's
discomfort. "Tell them they are mistaken," he said to the
guide. "I have no acquaintance with this god called Y'wa. Nor
do I have the slightest idea who their 'white brother' could
be." He returned to Rangoon leaving the Karen disappointed.[2] He recounted his story to his superior, Lieutenant
Colonel Michael Symes, who referred to it in his book, *An
Account of an Embassy to the Kingdom of Ava in the Year
1795*, published in 1827 in Scotland.

The English diplomat was followed in 1816 by a Muslim
traveller who entered a remote Karen village. Although not a

"white" man, he carried a holy book and the Karen wondered if he could be the one that they had been waiting for. He left a book, saying that it contained writings about God, and the Karens began to develop rituals venerating it.[3] But then the Christians missionaries came.

The Karens' traditional teachings are almost direct replicas of Genesis. As Donald Mackenzie Smeaton, a British missionary to the Karen in the nineteenth century, argues: "Their belief in the character and attributes of God is absolutely identical with the teachings of Christianity, and requires no modifications to make it a fully developed Christianity save the teachings of Jesus Christ as the Revelation of God and the Saviour of Man."[4] They believed in one God, named Y'wa – close to the Hebrew name Yawei – and this God was the creator of the universe. They believed that man had fallen away from Y'wa, by eating forbidden fruit. An ancient Karen poem claimed:

> Y'wa formed the world originally.
> He appointed food and drink.
> He appointed the "fruit of trial".
> He gave detailed orders.
> Mu-kaw-lee deceived two persons.
> He caused them to eat the fruit of the tree of trial.
> They obeyed not; they believed not Y'wa . . .
> When they ate the fruit of trial,
> They became subject to sickness, aging and death.[5]

According to a former missionary, Harry Ignatius Marshall, Y'wa told the man and woman he had created: "My son and daughter both, your father will make an orchard for you, and in that orchard there will be seven kinds of trees bearing seven kinds of fruit. Of the seven kinds there is one that is not good to eat. Do not partake of it. If you eat of it, you will fall ill; you will grow old; you will die. Do not eat it."[6]

But, as in the Garden of Eden, "the Devil, in the form of a great serpent, came and engaged them in conversation" and persuaded them to eat the fruit.[7] Initially the man was not convinced, but his wife, "Naw I-u", was seduced. She believed the serpent that the fruit would enable them to "ascend to heaven, to fly, and to burrow under the ground at will",[8] and so she ate the fruit. She persuaded her husband to try some. The next day, Y'wa came to visit the couple and "laid his curse upon them" for their disobedience.[9]

Karen poems also claimed that the "all-powerful" Y'wa had "the knowledge of all things" and had created man and woman. Y'wa created heaven and earth, and specifically, woman had been formed "from the rib of man".

Y'wa faced opposition from an evil power known as "Naw k'paw". This "Naw k'paw" had once been a servant of Y'wa but had been cast out for insulting the eternal God. Naw k'paw continues in the world, striving to deceive people and cause death and destruction. Harry Ignatius Marshall explains that in Karen legends, Naw k'paw "is the direct author of evil and of the curse that has fallen upon the earth".[10]

There has been much speculation and debate over how the Karens developed these poems and legends, so akin to the Old Testament. The Karens believe their people originated in Mongolia, in an area they refer to as Htee Hset Met Ywa, which means "Land of Flowing Sands". This is often taken to mean the area bordering the source of the Yangtsekiang river in the Gobi Desert in China. From there, they migrated south and were among the first settlers to enter Burma, in 739 BC. The Independent Karen Historical Research Association claims that the Karens left Mongolia in 2017 BC, migrated to East Turkistan where they stayed for 147 years, then to Tibet where they lived for 476 years, before going to Yunnan Province in southern China, and ending up in Burma.

Some suggest that the Karens were one of the lost tribes of Israel. If that is true, then they had got very lost – Kawthoolei is 4,000 miles from Jerusalem.[11] Some claim that the Karens must have been influenced by the Jews, but Richardson points out that while there are striking parallels with the Old Testament, nowhere in Karen poems and legends is there an equivalent to Abraham or Moses, two of the most important people in Judaism.[12]

It has also been suggested that the Karen met the Nestorian Christians in the eighth century AD. Smeaton is a proponent of this theory. "It appears most probable that their origin dates from the time when the Karens had not yet entered Burma, and that they were derived from the colony of Nestorian Jews who made their way by land from Armenia to China in the early Middle Ages, and whose track the Karens must have crossed in their journey southwards," claims Smeaton.[13] But Richardson believes this is unlikely, because if it had been so, they would surely have a story of the incarnation or a Redeemer dying and rising from the dead for our sins.[14]

Another theory is that Percoto, the Italian missionary who visited Burma in 1740, passed on the Old Testament stories to them. In Smeaton's view, there are two reasons why the idea that Percoto influenced the Karen is unlikely. Firstly, the Italian missionaries never reached as far as Karen territory – and even if they had, there would not have been enough time for the stories to have become such a part of Karen heritage before the American missionaries arrived in 1828. None of the stories were written – they were all either sung or recited from memory, having been passed from person to person and generation to generation.

Richardson believes the Karen poems and legends, with their extraordinary parallels with Genesis, are difficult to explain away in worldly terms. "Could it be that Karen beliefs about Y'wa predate both Judaism and Christianity? Did such beliefs spring from that ancient root of monotheism which characterised the age of the early patriarchs? The answer is almost certainly – yes!" he argues.[15] In which case, perhaps God had truly planted these seeds to prepare the Karen people for a direct relationship with Him.

Whatever the explanation, the background certainly made the missionaries' task easier. In the nineteenth century missionaries travelled to all parts of the world to win converts for Christ. They were following the instructions of the Great Commission set out in Matthew 28:18–20, where the eleven disciples met with Jesus on the mountain in Galilee. Jesus told them:

> "All authority in heaven and on earth has been given to me. Therefore go and make disciples of all nations, baptising them in the name of the Father and of the Son and of the Holy Spirit, and teaching them to obey everything I have commanded you. And surely I am with you always, to the very end of the age."

In many places, missionaries encountered resistance. Tribes in Africa and Asia resented foreigners arriving to persuade them to join a new religion, and many associated the missionaries with the less attractive aspects of colonialism and empire-building. In much of Burma, the missionaries had a tough time.

However, when the first missionaries reached the Karen, they were greeted with open arms. The Karen, following their ancient legend about the young white brother with the Golden Book, told the missionaries that they had been waiting for them for several hundred years. They were glad to get their book back.

The first missionary to the Karen was Adoniram Judson. Born in Massachusetts in the United States of America in 1788, Judson was the son of a Congregationalist minister. But in his teens he rebelled and abandoned the Christian faith. Studying at Providence College, now known as Brown University, he became more interested in intellectual pursuits than religion. Eugene Myers Harrison claims Judson "was enamoured of his brilliance and could not think of wasting his superb talents in so dull a calling as the ministry".[16] He saw himself "as a second Homer, writing immortal poems; as a second Alexander the Great" and, once he had graduated, he moved to New York to begin life as a playwright. "Judson was not only inordinately ambitious; he was also openly atheistic," Harrison writes.

Judson's parents were distraught. He had become close friends with a devout atheist, Jacob Eames, sometimes known as Ernest. Judson's morality became increasingly liberal and he turned into an exponent of infidelity. His intellectual powers were significant and he deployed them in arguments with his parents. He joined a troupe of actors on horseback through several states, and led what he later called "a wild, reckless life". A few weeks after joining the band, he left them on horseback. In an event that has Nativity undertones and was set to change the course of his life, Judson stopped one night at an inn. The landlord told him that the inn was almost full. The only room available was next to a young man who was dying. That did not faze him. "I'll take the room. Death has no terrors for me. You see, I'm an atheist."[17]

A sleepless night followed. The wall between the two rooms was thin and Judson was kept awake by the moans of a dying man. Judson wondered whether to go to the man, but felt there was nothing he could say or do to help. The man was clearly in agony and possessed by a fear of death. He shivered, covered himself and tried to sleep.

The next morning Judson inquired how the sick man was. The innkeeper told him the man had died. Judson asked who the man was, and he was told: "He was a graduate of

Providence College, a young fellow named Ernest."[18] It was Judson's best friend.

This experience shook Judson's atheism to the core. He went home to his parents and asked them to help him find a faith that would withstand life and death. In the midst of darkness, Judson turned to Scripture. He found a passage that was to become his hallmark, Ephesians 3:16–19:

> I pray that out of his glorious riches he may strengthen you with power through his Spirit in your inner being, so that Christ may dwell in your hearts through faith. And I pray that you, being rooted and established in love, may have power, together with all the saints, to grasp how wide and long and high and deep is the love of Christ, and to know this love that surpasses knowledge – that you may be filled to the measure of all the fullness of God.

In the final stages of his path to conversion, Judson decided to do the one thing he had purposefully wanted to avoid and went to Andover Theological College. After several months he overcame his remaining reservations about religion and dedicated his life to Christ. Soon afterwards, his interest in overseas mission work began to develop. "By day he was haunted by the vision of vast nations bound and dying in the darksome prison house of sin. By night he spent long, sleepless hours contemplating the hapless condition of teeming multitudes beyond the sea sinking into Christless graves," writes Harrison.[19]

However, he faced a hurdle. "As yet no American had ever considered missionary work except within the continent itself, and so no mission society existed to support him," according to a paper on *The Life and Work of Adoniram Judson*. But he read a book which made him determined to go abroad. It was Lieutenant Colonel Michael Symes' *An Account of an*

Embassy to the Kingdom of Ava 1795. In the absence of a missionary organisation to send him, Judson and some other seminarians, men of initiative, decided to establish one. It became known as the American Board.

In 1812 Judson and his wife Ann and another couple, Samuel and Harriet Newell, set sail for India.[20] During the journey they studied the New Testament in the original Greek, and Judson worked on a translation into English. As he studied, he was persuaded of the view that full immersion baptism was the biblical model, and for that reason he and his wife decided to change denominations and become Baptists. In Calcutta, they met with the British Baptist missionary, William Carey, and he and Ann were baptised by Carey's assistant, William Ward. They resigned from the Congregationalists and joined the American Baptists.

Judson and his wife moved on from India to Burma, despite Carey's attempts to dissuade him. The East India Company would not allow them to remain in India, and they did not wish to return to America. They therefore boarded a ship to Rangoon. Ann gave birth to her first baby, who died and had to be buried at sea. When they finally reached Rangoon, they were met, in Harrison's words, by the sight of "a squalid, unspeakably filthy village, whose uncivilised life had been utterly untouched and unsoftened by western influence."[21] They disembarked, but Ann was extremely ill and had to be carried in a stretcher.

The Judsons' time in Burma was eventful. Judson obtained a printer and press and started publishing New Testaments and tracts in Burmese. He developed a *zayat*, a Buddhist-style meditation room on a main street, where he could hold meetings and teach Burmese people the Gospel in a way which was not alien to them. This helped to break down barriers. After six years, they won their first convert, Maung Nau. Judson wrote in his diary on 27th June, 1819:

We proceeded to a large pond, the bank of which is graced with an enormous image of Buddha, and there administered baptism to Maung Nau, the first Burman convert. Oh may it prove the beginning of a series of baptisms in the Burman empire, which shall continue in uninterrupted succession to the end of time![22]

But their work was fraught with danger. Judson tried to appeal to the Emperor to allow religious freedom but the Burmese Emperor refused. This led to increased persecution of Christians. When war broke out between the British and the Burmese, as a result of Burmese raids on East India Company territory, Judson and other foreigners were imprisoned.[23] According to Harrison, "following the missionaries in their holy adventure, we behold scenes too horrible for words. On one occasion Judson, pitifully weak and emaciated, was driven in chains across the burning tropical sands, until, his back lacerated beneath the lash and his feet covered with blisters, he fell to the ground and prayed that the mercy of God might grant him a speedy death."[24] For almost two years he was jailed in terrible conditions, chained and in stocks. From his rat-infested cell he watched as other prisoners were taken out to be executed and wondered what his own fate would be.

Somehow Ann remained free, and gave birth to another child. Before his imprisonment, Judson had been translating the Bible into Burmese. Ann was instrumental in preserving the manuscripts from being destroyed. She hid them in a pillow, and brought the pillow to Judson in prison. "No one dreamed that the white man's head rested at night on the most precious of treasures – the Word of God."[25] When disaster almost struck and a jailer took the pillow for himself, Ann made a prettier pillow and offered it to the jailer in exchange for the original one. "Many times," writes Harrison, "smitten down with disease and at death's door, he breathed out the prayer, 'Lord let me finish my work. Spare me long enough to

put Thy saving Word into the hands of a perishing people.'
What a day of rejoicing it was when the Word of God came
off the press with its stupendous invitation: 'Whosoever will,
let him take the Water of Life freely'."[26]

Ann shared her husband's gift and passion for Bible trans-
lation, and learned the Thai language, then known as Siamese.
She became the first missionary to translate a portion of
Scripture, the Gospel of Matthew, into Thai.

In 1826 peace was restored, but Burma was more closed
than ever before. However, the Judsons persisted with their
missionary work. Although it was slow and challenging, they
never gave up. When a member of the Mission Board in
America wrote criticising their lack of conversions and enquir-
ing about the opportunities ahead, Judson replied: "The prospects are as bright as the promise of God."[27]

Judson reached the Karens on his travels around Burma, and
in 1828 the first Karen conversion took place. Ko Tha Byu had
been sold as a slave in a market in Moulmein, to a Burman
Christian. The Christian brought Ko Tha Byu to Judson and
asked Judson to share the Gospel with his slave. Ko Tha Byu
had been a bandit who had participated in about 30 murders
and was "a hardened criminal with a vicious nature and an
ungovernable temper".[28] But then he discovered the Bible, and
began to wonder if this was the lost Golden Book. Patiently
and prayerfully, Judson shared the love of Christ with this
former robber, and it began to make sense. Ko Tha Byu was
transformed, and became not only the first Karen convert, but
also their first missionary and evangelist, known as "the Karen
Apostle". He was baptised in Tavoy by Reverend George
Boardman.[29]

The conversion of Ko Tha Byu had a profound effect on the
Karen people. Their hearts were already prepared as a result
of their story of the Golden Book and the white brother and
so when Ko Tha Byu told his people that the white brother had

returned with the book that they had been expecting, hundreds of Karens converted. Within 25 years there were 11,878 baptised Karens.[30] By 1858, Karen Christians were starting missionary work themselves, to other hill tribes, such as the Kachin in northern Burma.[31] They found the Kachin just as receptive as they themselves had been, for the Kachin also had a monotheistic tradition and a legend of lost sacred writings. The Kachin and the Chin are now 90 per cent Christian.

For Judson, missionary work meant very simply an effort "to seek and to save the lost". One diary entry illustrates this:

> 11 March, The Lord's Day – Again took the main river. Soon came upon a boat full of men. Their chief, an elderly man, stated that he had already heard much of the gospel . . . We went to the shore and spent several hours very delightfully, under the shade of the overhanging trees and the banner of the love of Jesus . . . The old man went on his way, rejoicing aloud and declaring his resolution to make known the eternal God and the dying love of Jesus, all along the banks of the Yoon-za-len, his native stream.
> In these deserts let me labour,
> On these mountains let me tell
> How He died – The blessed Saviour,
> To redeem a world from hell.
> The banner of the love of Jesus,
> The dying love of Jesus!
> The redeeming love of the blessed Saviour![32]

After 33 years in Burma, he returned to the United States for his only ever furlough. His first wife, Ann, had died in Burma and he had married Sarah Boardman eight years later. In their eleven years together, they had eight children, three of whom died young. On his furlough, Judson married for the third time, to Emily Chubbuck, who returned with him to Burma for his final years.

As Judson lay dying, he referred frequently to his favourite theme, the love of Christ. "Oh the love of Christ! The wondrous love of Christ! The blessed efficacy of the love of Christ!" he said. "I have had such views of the loving condescension of Christ and the glories of Heaven, as I believe are seldom granted to mortal men. Oh, the love of Christ! It is the secret of life's inspiration and the source of Heaven's bliss. Oh the love of Jesus! We cannot understand it now, but what a beautiful study for eternity!"[33] He died in 1850, leaving 63 churches in Burma and 7,000 Christian converts. He was, as it is claimed in *The Life and Work of Adoniram Judson*, "indirectly responsible for the fulfilment of the Karen legends and provided for them their lost book, the Bible".

Judson was perhaps the best known missionary to Burma, and had a profound impact on the Karen through his conversion of Ko Tha Byu, but he was by no means the only missionary. Working alongside him in Burma and among the Karen were men like Jonathan Wade and Reverend Carpenter, who worked in Bassein. According to A.Q. Van Benschoten Jr, the mission centre in Bassein continued "under great difficulties of persecution".

Carpenter's attention subsequently turned to the Karens in Thailand. In 1873 he wrote in the *Baptist Missionary Magazine*: "Since the days of Boardman, the locale, numbers, and disposition of the Karen in Siam[34] toward the gospel have been subjects of frequent and deep interest to the Christian Karens and their missionaries in Burma."[35] His interest in Thailand was shared by Dr J.B. Vinton, a missionary based in Moulmein.

In the late 1870s Karens started to send their own missionaries to the Thai Karen communities. According to Dr McGilvary, the first Presbyterian missionary to northern Thailand, "two native Karens, ordained ministers, were sent by the American Baptist Mission to initiate in Lao territory a work among the Karens, a hill-people scattered sparsely throughout all the mountain region between Siam and Burma. The native evangelists brought with them letters from the missionaries in Burma, requesting us to aid them in getting Lao passports."[36]

McGilvary accompanied the Karen missionaries to a meeting with the new Prince in the area. "He very graciously gave direction to his brother to see that passports were issued, stating not only that the visitors were to be protected and aided as travellers, but also that they were to be allowed to teach the new religion, and that people were allowed to embrace it without fear." However, this was not to be. When the missionaries reached the first village, they were greeted with extreme hostility – and they found out that the Chao Uparat, a local king, had secretly dispatched a special messenger with a letter with his seal, forbidding any Karen subject to embrace Christianity. Anyone who did was to be reported to him. His letter reached the village before the edict of toleration was issued on 8th October, 1878.[37]

Two years later, in 1880, the Burma Baptist Convention decided to send three Karen evangelists to Thailand. The three, Maw Klo, Shwe Mya and Saw Kay, all came from Bassein. They went to Chiang Mai province in northern Thailand, and established one church there before returning to Burma a year later. Reverend Webster was dispatched by the Burma Baptist Convention to survey the work in Thailand, and on the way he baptised 70 people and established three more churches.[38]

In 1884, a Karen pastor returned to Burma from Thailand with a number of Thai Karen who wanted to study the Bible. One of these was Thra Mya Gaw, who graduated from the Karen Seminary in 1888 and returned to Thailand to pastor the Ban Nawk church, 30 miles north of Lampang.

By 1900 most of the Karen missionaries from Burma had returned home. Seven years later the Thai Karens gathered to send an appeal to the Burma Baptist Convention to send someone else to take charge of the Christian work among the Thai Karens. In 1909 Thra En Nay Dee Wah was sent to Thailand to lead the work among the Karens there, and in 1914 the Karen Baptist Convention of Burma sent a group of pastors to survey the work in Thailand. Another group came in 1929 and in 1932.

The missionary work among the Karens in Thailand stopped during the build up and duration of the Second World War, but after the war Burma became closed to missionaries and so the work in Thailand began in earnest. "We went to Thailand because we could not enter Burma to work among the Karen," writes A.Q. Van Benschoten Jr, who went to Thailand in 1951. "The Karen of Burma could not send any of their own people to work in Thailand. The Karen Convention in Burma asked the American Baptist Mission to send us here. We came as missionaries to the Karen in Thailand, though connected with the Burma Mission."[39]

Although it was not until the 1950s that missionaries were barred from Burma, Christians – especially among the Karen – had been persecuted for decades, ever since they first started to convert. Dr San C Po, one of the Karen leaders in the early twentieth century, said that the oppression of the Karens at the hands of the Burmans had been taking place for years, but it intensified with the arrival of Christianity. "The lot of the Karens under Burmese rule had been hard enough, but when the Burmans, made anxious by the rumours of war to be declared between Burma and Great Britain, heard that the Karens were taking up the Christian religion, they proceeded to make life unbearable for the new converts to Christianity. Persecution, religious and political, began in earnest," he writes in his book *Burma and the Karens*, first published in 1928. "Karens were caught and thrown into prison, suffering untold agonies, and a few were crucified."[40]

Klaw Meh, according to Dr San C Po, was nailed to a cross. A gruesome description follows. "The abdomen ripped open with intestines hanging down, which the crows were picking while the poor man writhed in agony in an impossible attempt to drive away the crows. His voice gradually grew weaker until at last he died a martyr on the cross like his Master, Jesus Christ, whom he had lately embraced."[41] This incident was witnessed by the Reverend Dr T Thanbyah, who wept every time he passed the place where the crucifixion was carried out.

Oppression of the Christian Karens sometimes took a less violent form. In one incident, according to Dr San C Po, "the pastors and elders of a Karen village once came down to Bassein and reported a matter relating to their Township Officer who, it seems, had gone to their village on a Sunday while a prayer meeting was in progress and ordered the villagers to come out and help carry his luggage to a *dak* bungalow. The pastor and elders were in a dilemma, for if ever a nation has a high regard for a religious service it is the Karen Christians. To be called away from prayers, especially when threatened by a Government official, the threats not unmingled with abuses, was indeed an awkward situation."[42]

But the persecution was matched, in Dr San C Po's view, by the blessings of Christianity and the progress which the missionaries brought to the Karen people. "The educational, social and spiritual progress of the Karens has been due, to a very large extent, to the missionaries who have so faithfully and sympathetically worked among and with them," he writes.[43] "The Karens are not ashamed or afraid to proclaim to the world publicly or in private that they owe what progress and advancement they have made to the missionaries."

One of the most important contributions of the missionaries was the development of a written script for the Karen. Until the missionaries came, the Karen language had no written form. In 1853, Dr Francis Mason completed a translation of the Bible in Sgaw Karen language, while Dr Jonathan Wade published dictionaries and a grammar of both the Sgaw and Pwo dialects.[44] The Bible was translated into Pwo Karen by the Reverend D.L. Brayton, and the Reverend J.G. Binney founded a Karen Theological Seminary in Moulmein in 1845. A Baptist college in Rangoon, which became Judson College in memory of the first missionary, was established in 1875. Translations of *Pilgrim's Progress,* the *Arabian Nights* and some Shakespeare plays have also been published in Karen.[45]

Perhaps as a result of the missionaries' work, the Karen placed – and continue to place today – huge value on education. According to Marshall, even before the British had established a government in Burma, an American missionary had set up a school in Moulmein which took in pupils who had walked hundreds of miles through the jungle by night, too frightened to risk walking by day, in order to learn to read the Bible in their own language. "The number of mission and Government schools began to increase rapidly," writes Marshall. "Every Christian church had its accompanying school, and in recent years many, if not most, of the non-Christian villages have come to have their schools also."

The fruit of the missionaries' work, built on the Karens' own traditional beliefs, has been enormous. Even though over half of Karen people today are still not Christians, Christianity has shaped much of Karen culture and much of their struggle for political freedom. It has also left numerous courageous Karen missionaries and evangelists working among their people today.

One such person is a man called Pastor Winai. Born in the jungle in Papung, across the Salween River from the Thai town of Mae Sariang, in 1952, Winai has lived his entire life in the Karen resistance. His father died soon after he was born and he lived for several years with his mother in the jungle. His mother died in 1971, and three years later he went to Bible school in Insein, Rangoon. In 1978, he came to Thailand and began preaching the Gospel in Thailand. He married a Thai Karen.

Winai had a vision to start a hostel to care for children. In 1982 he began this ministry with 30 children. All he had was 2,000 Thai Baht a month (£33). He was able only to afford one tin of sardines and a kilo of chilli to feed 30 children each day. But the support grew, the number of children grew to 82, and he lived by faith. "I said to my wife: 'If we don't have faith, we cannot do anything'."

In addition to looking after children, Winai founded a Karen church in Maesot, Thailand in 1994, and started a new hostel outside Maesot, which began with nine children and now has 64.

"I have a vision to build many churches for the Karen in Thailand," he says. "In Tak province there are more than 600 Karen villages. I am praying for the budget. But if we start the work, God will provide. Jesus told his disciples to go, without money, without belongings. Jesus told the story of how two talents became five. So we pray for such a blessing."

Although the Baptist missionaries were the most active, and as a result most Karen Christians are Baptists, there are other denominations represented, particularly the Seventh Day Adventists, Anglicans and Roman Catholics. One inspiring Karen Catholic priest is Saw Doh Soe, who works with the "True Life in God" mission on the Thai–Burmese border. His ministry is to provide higher education to some of the young Karen refugees who, although they receive primary and secondary education in the camps, often have little opportunity beyond that. "Once they pass tenth standard in the camp, only those who have contact with foreigners have a chance to be supported and go to university in Thailand," Saw Doh Soe told me. "But the grassroots with no outside contact have nowhere to go. I decided to do something for them."

Saw Doh Soe was ordained as a priest in 1981, but that had not been his original desire. Despite being raised in a Catholic family, his first ambition was to join the Burma Army. He believed that the Karen people were suffering as a result of the war, caused in his view by both the Burma Army and the Karen resistance. "So I decided to join the Burma Army to fight the Karen insurgents!" he said. "I believed we suffered more from the insurgents. They would come into a village, and the next day the Burma Army would come and torture and persecute the villagers." But while his application for military training was accepted, his parish priest stepped in. "He didn't allow me to join the army. He sent me to seminary in Bassein instead!"

For two years after his ordination, Saw Doh Soe served as a parish priest, and then worked as the rector of a seminary. After another stint in a parish, in 1995 he left Burma and served as a seafarers' chaplain in Bangkok. Four years later, he was appointed by his bishop to conduct a survey of the Karen refugee situation. "I knew nothing about it when I started the survey on the border," he said.

Now he serves as a refugee chaplain, and provides a three-year course, open to people regardless of religion, in which he seeks to combine spiritual and practical education. He focuses on both the head and the heart. "Unless there is purification of the heart, nothing new can be received," he said. "Their hatred, spirit of revenge, rebellion will remain. They have often witnessed villages burned down, parents killed. I want to help them clean up their bad feelings from those experiences – otherwise this war will continue, generation by generation." His course includes English, Burmese, mathematics, history, geography, but also Bible study and prayer. He has Catholics, Baptists, Buddhists and Animists in his classes, but he does not compromise his own faith in God. "I see the person as a person," he told me. "No one is perfect. Everybody has some misconduct, some wrongdoing. That helps me to accept everyone and forgive them, and to be able to help them."

Daeng R, writing in a publication called *The Karens' Struggle for Human Rights*, summarises the impact of Christianity on the Karen with these observations:

> One impression of Kawthoolei which remains deeply with me is the dedication of so many of their people to the Christian religion . . . But there is something strange about their Christian faith which I could not quite identify. Perhaps the problem is that I have become accustomed to Christians in the West who so seriously use Christianity to try to justify everything they do . . . When Captain Kanami, my guide, called the group together for prayer before my departure, I expected him to talk about God being on the side of the Karens and therefore proving that their struggle was just. I expected him to pray for guidance and protection in their fight against the Burmese. But I was mistaken. In their prayer meetings they thanked God for fellowship together, for strength to serve the people and for the simple food and clothing they had. Never did they attempt to justify their struggle by claiming God as being on their side, nor did they ever use Christianity as a way to condemn the Burmese. Perhaps I do not yet fully understand the Christian faith but I found in this a strange and uplifting attraction to it.

NOTES

1 The DKBA was formed in 1995 as a breakaway faction of the Karen, siding with the SPDC. See Chapter Five for further explanation.

2 Don Richardson, *Eternity in their Hearts*, p. 75

3 Ibid., p. 76

4 Donald Mackenzie Smeaton, *The Loyal Karens of Burma*, p. 178

5 As quoted by Don Richardson, *Eternity in their Hearts*, p. 78

6   Harry Ignatius Marshall, *The Karen People of Burma*, p. 215

7   Ibid., p. 215

8   Ibid., p. 215

9   Ibid., p. 215

10 Ibid., p. 213

11 Richardson, p. 83

12 Ibid., p. 83

13 Smeaton

14 Richardson, p. 83

15 Ibid., p. 84

16 Eugene Myers Harrison, *Apostle of the Love of Christ in Burma*, originally published in *Giants of the Missionary Trail*, Scripture Press, 1954.

17 Ibid.

18 Ibid.

19 Ibid.

20 *The Life and Work of Adoniram Judson, Missionary to Burma*

21 Harrison

22 as quoted by Eugene Myers Harrison

23 *The Life and Work of Adoniram Judson, Missionary to Burma*

24 Harrison

25 Ibid.

26 Ibid.

27 Ibid.

28 Ibid.

29 A.Q. Van Benschoten Jr, *A Thailand Missionary: The Story of the Karen in Thailand*

30 Robert Bradshaw, *The Life and Work of Adoniram Judson, Missionary to Burma*, published on his website, www.theologicalstudies.org.uk/article_judson.html

31 Richardson, p. 96

32 Harrison
33 Ibid.
34 The former name for what is now Thailand
35 Van Benschoten Jr
36 Ibid.
37 Ibid.
38 Ibid.
39 Ibid.
40 Dr San C Po, *Burma and the Karens,* p. 2
41 Ibid., p. 2
42 Ibid., p. 14
43 Ibid., p. 58
44 Marshall, p. 300
45 Ibid, p. 310

CHAPTER TWO

LOYALTY BETRAYED

"Greater love has no one than this,
that he lay down his life for his friends"
John 15:13

Micah Rollings[1] sat in a chair in Pastor Simon's house in Mae
La refugee camp, and laughed. He had shaved all his hair off
and was completely bald. Aged in his eighties, his hearing had
almost totally gone, but he could still read and speak – indeed,
his mind was extremely sharp – so I wrote questions down and
he answered them. He recalled his own experiences fighting
alongside the Allies in the Second World War, and then his
years in the Karen struggle for freedom.

"Why were the Karens so loyal to the British in the Second
World War?" he read out loud from the piece of paper on
which I had scribbled my first question.

"A good question," he said. He thought for a few seconds.
"Because we were foolish!"

Ever since the British first came across the Karens in the
mid-nineteenth century, the Karens displayed extraordinary
loyalty to their colonial rulers. Donald Mackenzie Smeaton, a
missionary in Burma in the nineteenth century, described the
Karen as "the staunchest and bravest defenders of British
rule" and, he adds, during the three Anglo-Burmese wars,

"but for the loyalty and courage of the Karens, the rebel Burmans and the Shans would, in all probability, have overrun Lower Burma".[2] The Karens, Smeaton continues, "are at heart loyal to us and they have proved their loyalty by freely shedding their blood in defence of our rule and in the cause of order".[3]

A.G. Campagnac took the same view. "Thousands of them have embraced Christianity, the religion to which their ancient traditions pointed; and Christian people of whatever nationality are not aliens to them, nor is a British Government an administration of foreigners," he wrote. "Christianity had taken a great hold of their minds and hearts. They are as a body, a truthful, guileless people. They are keenly sensitive to the smallest harshness or to injustice, but they are also intensely appreciative of the smallest token of kindness of friendliness. In earliest times their intuitive loyalty to the sovereign they take pride in calling their 'Great Good Queen' was inspiring." Loyalty to the British Empire, he adds, "is ingrained in their very constitution, and fidelity to the King-Emperor is a duty, sacred and religious".[4]

Their loyalty came to the fore in the Second World War, but that was certainly not the beginning of it, nor was it the only time the Karens made sacrifices for the British Empire. It was in 1826, when they served as guides to the British forces in the expedition against Ava, that their relationship with the British began. Major Snodgrass, the commander of that operation, praised the Karens for their reliability.[5] In the Second Anglo-Burmese War, from 1852–53, which, as Smeaton describes, resulted in the annexation by the British of all of Lower Burma and the addition of Burma as a province of British India, the Karens aided the British against the Burmans. Once again they served as guides to the invaders, who seized control of the Shwe Dagon Pagoda, one of the most significant targets, near Rangoon.[6]

The Burmans knew the Karens were assisting the British, and the relationship between the two ethnic groups deteriorated. The origins of the ethnic hatred today can be traced back to the Anglo-Burmese War years. After the capture of Shwe Dagon Pagoda, the Burmans sought revenge on the Karens, burning all Karen villages within 50 miles of Rangoon, seizing and destroying rice supplies, and murdering hundreds of people.[7]

In 1914 when the First World War broke out, the Karen people applied in large numbers to join the British military forces. In the Burma Rifles, for example, out of 16 companies, three were Karen. They were represented in other regiments too.[8]

But it was for their courage and sacrifice in the Second World War that the British owe the Karen the greatest debt of gratitude. In December 1941, the Japanese forces attacked British and American bases in Burma and on Christmas Day, Rangoon was bombed. The Japanese had already swept through Malaya and Singapore, and had reached Burma through Thailand. The British were unprepared and short of men – in contrast to the Japanese, they did not know how to fight in the jungle. They relied on motorised vehicles which broke down in rough conditions, while the Japanese used bicycles.[9] But the Karens and other ethnic groups came to their aid. By the closing stages of the war it is estimated that as many as 50,000 Karen were serving with the Allied forces.[10] According to the journalist John Pilger, an estimated 16,000 British and Allied forces died on the Burma–Siam railway, but over 100,000 Burmese of different ethnic backgrounds, including Karens, died. In Thailand today there are two cemeteries at Kanchanaburi where thousands of British soldiers are buried. There is no cemetery or memorial for the Karens who gave their lives.

The war in Burma took various turns, and in 1942 the British were in retreat. They withdrew to India. The Japanese, supported by the Burma Independence Army, exacted their revenge on those who had supported the British, including the Karen. But Prime Minister Winston Churchill and his commanders in the Far East were working on plans to re-invade Burma. Churchill appointed Colonel Orde Wingate as the Special Forces Commander, and the "Chindits", named after a mythical beast found outside Burmese Buddhist temples, was formed with British and Indian troops along with the Karen, Kachin, Chin and other hill tribes. The Chindits were sometimes known as "Wingate's Raiders".

Wingate, a devout Christian with a passion for the Old Testament, became an admirer of the Karens' fighting skills and loyalty, and in turn he became popular with the Karen troops because he listened to them and appointed senior Karen advisers. They were amazed to see him in action in the frontline. One former Karen Chindit, Pu Htun Tin, said: "Wingate was a brave leader and so worthy of our praise."[11] The Chindits adopted the Karens' jungle warfare tactics, using elephants to transport the troops and their equipment.

With the 14th Army, backed up by the Chindits, the British slowly made some dents in the Japanese armoury. On 23rd February, 1942, with two-thirds of their troops on the wrong side of the river, the British blew up the bridge over the Sittang River to halt the progression of the Japanese. In 1943, the Chindits crossed the Chindwin River and severed Japanese communications on the railway from Mandalay to Myitkyina. By 1944, the Chindits were in control of several sections of the railway.

Another division was the Special Operational Executive or "SOE", founded in 1940 primarily for the Allied Forces in Europe. It was a secretive organisation combining guerrilla warfare with espionage. "In March 1938 when Hitler's annexation of his Austrian homeland made imminent danger plain, the British began afresh to turn some official attention towards irregular and clandestine warfare," writes M.R.D. Foot in *The SOE in France*.[12] This meant industrial and military sabotage, labour agitation and strikes, continuous propaganda, terrorist acts against traitors and German leaders, and boycotts and riots. "We need absolute secrecy, a certain fanatical enthusiasm, willingness to work with people of different nationalities, complete with political reliability," said Minister of Economic Warfare, Hugh Dalton.[13] The SOE was born.

A component of the SOE and a key element of the operation to remove the Japanese from Burma was Force 136, an elite unit of the secret service. Force 136 had a spider web as its symbol, signifying a trap to ensnare the enemy, and it was engaged in guerrilla warfare, sabotage training and intelligence work. When the British retreated to India in 1942, one Force 136 soldier, Major Hugh Seagrim, decided to stay behind, and his superiors agreed. Seagrim has become one of the Karens' heroes as a result.

General Bo Mya, who went on to become the leader of the KNU resistance forces in the Karens' struggle against Burman oppression, worked closely with Seagrim. When the British retreated to India, the Japanese started recruiting Karens to join their police force. Some of the Karen who were close to Seagrim were recruited, and they asked Seagrim what they should do. According to Bo Mya, Seagrim told them they had to do it, in order to survive. "If you cannot survive, I cannot survive," was his message. So Bo Mya and others worked for the Japanese police, but revealed nothing to their new masters about Seagrim's whereabouts. Seagrim, Bo Mya recalls, "loved the British and the Karen. He did not leave for India, because he loved the Karen."

Seagrim recruited 3,000 Karen volunteers and lived among the Karen, who hid him from the Japanese for two years in the jungle. General Tamla Baw, another leader of the Karen resistance against the Burmans from the end of the Second World War to the present day, knew Seagrim personally. "Major Seagrim had great confidence in our Karen people. He trusted us completely, and seemed to be very honest with us," he recalled. Seagrim wore Karen dress and ate Karen food along with everyone else.[14]

A committed Christian, Seagrim always carried a Bible under his arm. In a biography of Seagrim, called *Grandfather Longlegs*, Ian Morrison writes: "Even more than his character and personality, it was this religious side to Seagrim's nature, his Christianity, which made such a deep and lasting impression on the Karens. They had known American missionaries. Americans, in the minds of these simple people, were either teachers or pastors. Englishmen were either officials who administered the country or business men who made money. They had never known an Englishman, let alone an officer in the British Army, who read the Bible and liked to talk about Christianity with them and prayed each evening and exhorted them to find strength through prayer."[15]

One of his closest Karen friends was Ta Roe, and Seagrim regularly sought to encourage him in times of trouble. "We must not be downcast, Ta Roe," he told him on one occasion. "We are Christians. After the war, I don't want to go on being a soldier. I want to become a missionary and work amongst the Karens. I have lived with them now so long that I would like to go on living with them always. I want to devote my life to the Karens."[16]

Seagrim was joined at one point by some British parachutists, including Major Nimmo and Major McCrindle, and they worked to develop communications back to India and start reconnaissance in Rangoon. Some of the Karen Force 136 agents, and ordinary villagers, were dispatched to Rangoon to gather information on the Japanese movements. These were men like Bo Po Hla.

Unfortunately the Japanese had already become suspicious because every time Po Hla and others returned from a trip to Rangoon, the British had been able to bomb the Japanese with extraordinary precision. So the Japanese arrested Po Hla, and sent 2,000 troops up to the Karen hills to investigate. Bo Mya was interrogated, but denied seeing "the white man". Other Karen also refused to give Seagrim up. Many were beaten, tortured and killed. By the end of 1943, over 270 Karen had been killed and the Japanese vowed to kill at least one thousand until Seagrim gave himself up.[17] Eventually some of the Karen showed the Japanese the camp where Seagrim had been. The Japanese surrounded the place, and shot one British officer. Seagrim, however, had escaped.

In a hurry to escape Seagrim had stepped on a sharp piece of bamboo, and cut himself. There was a trail of blood, and for a while the Japanese thought he was dead. In the beginning of May 1944, they started to pull back their troops, but they continued to beat and torture the Karen.

But when Seagrim heard of the suffering they were enduring, he knew it was because of him. He could not bear it any more, and decided to give himself up. He sent Pa An to the Karens to tell them he would surrender, because he did not want them to be tortured any more. Pa An returned to Seagrim, and confirmed that people were being slaughtered. "The conditions were critical," said Bo Mya. Seagrim's decision was made. He sent Pa An to talk to the Japanese. He told them he was one of Seagrim's men, and they accused him of lying. "You don't look like a soldier," they said. He assured them he was, and so the Japanese moved troops up to the hills to capture Seagrim. As he gave himself up, Seagrim pleaded with the Japanese to spare the Karen and take him alone, but they ignored his request.

Six Karen were taken with him, including Pa An. "Even though he was British, Seagrim thought of himself as a Karen," says Bo Mya. "When he surrendered he wore a Karen costume. The Japanese asked him to take it off and he refused."

They were held in jail for a short time, and then in September 1944, they were all shot. Before their deaths Seagrim was permitted to conduct a short service in jail. According to another officer, "nothing could reveal better this man's wonderful character than those words which are now lost. A tribute to the dead, a prayer for the living and, greatest of all, a word for his cruel captors, for of the Japs he said, in the words of Christ, 'Lord, forgive them, for they know not what they do.' "[18]

In 1944 preparations for the re-invasion of Burma by the British were underway. Six months after Seagrim's death, Force 136 parachuted in 50 agents and dropped supplies of arms and food which the hill tribes had been waiting for. About 2,000 Karen collected the supplies. Lieutenant-Colonel Cromarty-Tulloch was on the ground to receive the extra forces, and when Alexander Boal, a Force 136 officer, parachuted in he was met by Tulloch dressed in silk pyjamas and wearing a monocle.

Bo Mya remembers the night the British parachutists landed. "There was a full moon and I could see clearly everywhere," he says. "We saw aeroplanes flying close to the trees. I looked around and saw one plane. I saw parachutes coming out of the back. Early in the morning I went to the field where they dropped the parachutes. I saw British soldiers hiding packages in the forest. They did not know I was in the Japanese police."

After assisting the British soldiers in hiding their supplies, Bo Mya went back to his village. The Japanese arrived half an hour later. They asked about the aeroplanes and Bo Mya said that he had seen them. He told the Japanese that he and the other Karen had been to search for the British but had not found anyone.

The British were hiding supplies near the house of another Karen who worked for the Japanese police. The Japanese wanted to go to this house and search in the vicinity for the British, but Bo Mya told them he was tired and wanted to sleep. They allowed him to rest, while they moved on.

The next day, two British parachutists who had lost their way arrived in Bo Mya's village at eight o'clock in the morning, and said that their company had dispersed and they were lost. They were looking for other British troops. But there were two Japanese commanders in the village at the time the two British officers arrived, and so the two British men moved on swiftly.

In each village, the British recruited Karen villagers to their cause. When asked if they would join the British Army, the Karens response was usually: "We will only follow you if you fight to win. If you fight only halfway, we won't." The British promised that this time they would not retreat and leave the Karens to the mercy of the Japanese. On the first day alone, 500 Karens were recruited, according to Bo Mya. By day two, 1,000 Karens had been added to the British forces.

In December 1944, the British re-invasion began in earnest with a race for Toungoo. The Japanese wanted to capture Toungoo in order to protect Rangoon, but to reach the town they had to go through Karen territory. The Karen, using their knowledge of the jungle, set numerous traps called *ponjis*, stout bamboo laths sharpened to a very dangerous point. Japanese were impaled on them one by one. General Slim's account of what happened is as follows:

> . . . The Japanese . . . made for Toungoo, and it looked as if they might beat us to it. But I still had a short in my locker for them. . . . Their way led them through the country of the Karens, a race which had remained staunchly loyal to us even in the blackest days of Japanese occupation. . . . It was not at all difficult to get the Karens to rise against the hated Japanese; the problem was to

restrain them from rising too soon. But now the time had come, and I gave the word, "Up the Karens!" Japanese, driving hard through the night down jungle roads for Toungoo, ran into ambush after ambush; bridges were blown ahead of them, their foraging parties massacred, their sentries stalked, their staff cars shot up. Air-strikes, directed by British officers, watching from the ground the fall of each stick of bombs, inflicted great damage. . . . They lost the race for Toungoo.[19]

Although Rangoon fell to the 14th Army on 3rd May, 1945 with almost no resistance, the Karen were then confronted with the sight of 50,000 Japanese troops in retreat across their land. The fight continued until September 1945, a month after Japan had formally surrendered, and the Karens killed at least 12,500 Japanese in what was the most successful guerrilla campaign against the Japanese of the entire Second World War.[20] The Karens killed more Japanese in Burma than all the Allied armies put together.

Major Ian Abbey was with Force 136 and was one of the parachutists who landed in the Dali Forest, east of Moulmein. He and his 20 soldiers were dropped on 29th March, 1945, in Mepale Valley near to Kawkareik Township. He is in no doubt about the crucial role the Karen played in the effort. "Our lives depended on them. We wouldn't have stood a chance without them."

"After I landed, I was sitting there without any food and without much water, in the jungle. I wondered what on earth to do next," Major Abbey recalls. His supply containers had landed in some trees and were irretrievable, and he had lost his wireless equipment. "Then I heard some voices on the path, and two Karen people saw me. They took me under their wing, brought me to a village, provided food."

Saw Ta Po was one of the two Karens who met the Force 136 troops, and took them to Ger Gaw village. Major Abbey established a base camp in the Dali Forest near the village, but had to keep moving because the Japanese became aware of his presence. They moved to Ler Bo Kee, but then had to move again, this time to Shanywathit. But each time he and his men moved, a Karen village was always on hand to provide shelter and protection. In Shanywathit, Bo Aung Shin greeted them and provided food and help. "They did not betray us to the Japanese. When the Japanese got to know we were there, we moved on. The Karen passed us from village to village. They brought us food and intelligence. We were surrounded by the Japanese, and it would have only taken one Karen to lead the Japanese to us. I could have been betrayed at any time. But the Karen did not betray us."

In fact, so enthusiastic were the Karen in support of the British that Major Abbey faced the challenge of restraining them. "One of my biggest problems was to prevent the Karens, who we had given arms and ammunition, from engaging in battle before the time was ready."

One of Major Abbey's group, Captain Tony Bennett, agrees. "We trusted them with our lives," he said. "That's why we owe them so much." He recalls the Karens' Christian faith as being central to their behaviour. After being sheltered in the Dali Forest by a man named Saw Ku, when the time came for the soldiers to leave the local Karens held a "farewell sing-song-cum-prayer-meeting". Major Abbey sang Blake's "Jerusalem", which Saw Ku followed with a mouth-organ solo. "Saw Ku then made a long speech in which he said that he didn't have much time nowadays to be a good Christian but he was still one at heart . . . ," Captain Bennett wrote in his diary. "We have two pastors among our levies and he does all he can to support them. There are two services of a Sunday and sometimes prayers at roll call in the evening."

In Shanywathit, Major Abbey sent a letter to Saw Po Htain, who served in the Thaton reserve, requesting wireless sets in order to communicate with headquarters in Calcutta. The party then moved through more villages before reaching Kya-in, where they sought and received help from young Karen who could speak English, to act as interpreters.

By June 1945, the Japanese were on the heels of the parachutists, and so they had to leave Kya-in and head for Metala village. While they escaped the brutality of the Japanese, the local villagers were not so fortunate. The Japanese besieged the parachutists' deserted camp in the Dali Forest, and attacked the nearest village, Kalagon. Several hundred villagers, mainly Indian Muslims, were slaughtered, including women and children, and their homes burned down. On 6th August, the Japanese caught up with the parachutists in Metala, but again Major Abbey and his men escaped narrowly. The village rice supplies were destroyed, however, and villagers tortured as a punishment for feeding and harbouring the British.

Captain Bennett described the horrors that the Karen and other ethnic groups suffered for their allegiance to the Allies. One particular village of Arakanese had been tireless in providing the British with information. "The help this village gave us led to an appalling tragedy for them," Captain Bennett wrote in his diary. "Somehow or other the Japanese found out about it, and a short while before the war ended, when we were miles away in another area, they went to exact retribution. The men returned from Moulmein to find the village destroyed and all those in it dead. Old men, women and children had been stuffed down the village well, some of them not yet dead."

Major Abbey and his men made it through several more villages before the end of the war, reaching Kya-in on 17th September, where they attended a victory reception. On arrival in Kya-in village, as the war was almost over and people were beginning to consider the future political arrangements for Burma, Major Abbey was greeted by the village leaders. One of the elders then gave a speech, in which he expressed support for the British effort:

> On behalf of the Karen people of Kya-in and the neighbouring village tracts, I extend to you our heartiest welcome to our village . . . You, sirs, as British officers, we look up to you as symbols of freedom, strength and inspiration and offer to you our heartfelt gratitude for the part you have valiantly and nobly played for the sake of peace and humanity. From the bottom of our hearts, we unreservedly extend to you our hearths and home for your rest and recuperation.

He then appealed for continued British support:

"We have dearly paid for our unswerving loyalty to the benign British Crown, especially the Christian section of our community, which has continuously been under suspicion and surveillance of the Japanese, our erstwhile enemy."

He detailed the looting, pillaging and killing carried out by the Burmans in alliance with the Japanese, after the British had retreated in 1942. He claimed that his villagers had been taken for forced labour by the Japanese, for use on the construction of the Burma–Thailand Railway as well as for mining and timber work.

Saw Lincoln Ja was one of many Karen taken for forced labour by the Japanese. Named after Abraham Lincoln, he noted that his namesake "freed people from moral and physical slavery". According to Hamilton Walters, as a forced labourer Saw Lincoln Ja "cleared jungles, levelled ground and constructed airfields", and witnessed the deaths of some labourers after contact with the sap of the Thuu Tee tree, which caused boils and blisters all over their body.[21]

"Pages would not suffice to record genuine incidents of horror and gruesome tales of woe during the painful era of face-slapping, intimidation and servitude," the headman told Major

Abbey. "An able artist would paint a better picture of the Japanese works of devastation and present you with a graphic and vivid account of attendant raping, pestilence and mounted death-tolls of both labour and war prisoners, and would also spread before you a canvas depicting naked humanities."

In a direct appeal for independence, the village leader referred to the Burmans' "open hostility against the Karen race", depicted in the massacres of Karens at Myaungmya and Papun, and the Burmans' "overt Herculean efforts" to live outside the British Commonwealth. "These two facts must, in our submission, serve as food for thought for the British Parliament to review the previous Constitution of Burma in shaping its future destiny. We make bold to state that we have come to a parting of ways with the Burmans, whence we prefer to prepare our own destiny in the British Commonwealth of Nations."

He gave a warning of things to come. "As a minority, our political union with the Burman in the past under the guise of democracy has not been a safe, satisfactory and happy one. History repeats itself. Centuries ago, before the advent of British rule, our ancestors had continuously suffered persecution at the hands of the Burmans and no sooner had the British left this shore for war strategy, then the tell-tale temperament of the Burman made itself felt on the Karen masses . . . We strongly appeal through you Sir, to the authorities concerned, that the Karens be allotted a certain part of Burma where we could, under the guidance and care of the British Government, in the first instance administer ourselves free from the Burman."

Such requests had already been made by Karens before the war. In 1921, the Whyte Committee was formed to examine proposals for political reform in Burma, and Dr San C Po appealed for autonomy or independence for the Karens. "It is their desire to have a country of their own, where they may

progress as a race and find the contentment they seek . . .
'Karen Country', how inspiring it sounds!" he wrote.[22] He
warned that if the Karens were not given at least autonomy,
within a federal Burma, "it is greatly to be feared that a new
group or generation of Karen extremists or obstructionists
will arise".[23] He argued that it was "absolutely necessary for
the good of all concerned that a division or separation of
administration of the [Karen] province be established".[24]

Another British soldier involved in working with the Karen
in the final stages of the war was Colonel Michael Osborn,
second-in-command of the first battalion of the West
Yorkshire Regiment. He had already served in the Battle of
Keren in Eritrea, for which he was awarded the Military
Cross, and in the Western Desert, for which he won the
Distinguished Service Order, and he was to go on to be mili-
tary secretary to General Slim when Prime Minister Clement
Attlee appointed him Chief of the Imperial General Staff.

Colonel Osborn recalls setting up camp north of Rangoon,
but soon received fresh instructions to go to Moulmein in
southern Burma. "We had to travel overland, which entailed
crossing the Salween River, which by then had had all its
bridges demolished and was in flood," he said. "This was
quite a task to get a battalion of 800 men across. But eventually we accomplished it, and went a few miles into the jungle
north of Moulmein."

He then divided his men in two, and took command of half
the battalion. With his 400 men, they had to "comb the
ground up as far as the Thai border" looking for the Japanese.
"Our instructions were to take the surrender of Japanese soldiers who had been given their orders to surrender but in
many cases hadn't and had kept in the deep jungle. We also
had to get as far as the Thai border to help in the operation of
disbanding the notorious Siamese railway. That involved
rounding up the Japanese. In fact I never got as far as that

because it took us much longer to make our way through the deep jungle."

To do this, Colonel Osborn made contact with the Karen. "The Karen started welcoming us with open arms. This was my first opportunity to meet those splendid people for whom I have had a deep admiration ever since," he explained. In order to solicit their help, he built relationships with them, in the same way Seagrim had done. "It was no good just arriving in a village one night, talking to the headman, and then carrying on the next morning. It needed at least a three or four day stop," he said.

These stops often involved some adventurous meals. In one village, Colonel Osborn and four officers joined the headman for dinner, along with a dozen Karen. "We were all sitting cross-legged on the ground with a table cloth with great bowls of rice," he remembers. "I was given a very generous helping. Then through the interpreter I said to the headman how much I was enjoying the rice, but I wondered what these black things were. The interpreter and the headman talked for about five minutes before the interpreter eventually turned to me and said 'leeches'. I nearly died! Leeches were the one bad memory of the Burmese jungle – we were forever stopping to remove them with a cigarette. The interpreter discussed the matter with the headman, and then turned back to me to enquire: 'Oh, you've never eaten them before?' I said they were lovely!"

He received other generous hospitality from his Karen hosts. One night at dinner, the village headman offered Colonel Osborn 60 bananas on a branch. The bananas were put in a corner of the Colonel's hut. "My batman rigged up some kind of bed with a mosquito net, and a packing case as a bedside table, and he went outside and promptly fell asleep. He snored the whole night. I fell asleep but woke up in the middle of the night, with the moon filtering through the trees, to see something flying into my mosquito net," he recalls. "I stretched my hand out under the net to my revolver, and I switched on my torch, but immediately switched it off again and thought 'What on earth am I going to do?' The whole place was a mass of bats, all gorging themselves on the bananas! I shouted to my batman but he went on snoring. I managed to get back to sleep, but the next morning there wasn't a banana left. I told the headman and he burst out laughing."

The Colonel's rapport with the headman grew when a peacock walked past them as they were talking. The headman explained that the peacock is a sacred bird for the Buddhists. But, he added, "It's very good to eat." Being a keen hunter, Colonel Osborn expressed interest. "I wouldn't mind having a shot," he said. The headman arranged a Karen tracker and they went down the path into the jungle. "Suddenly the Karen tracker signalled me to stop. He said 'Don't shoot.' I thought 'Oh no, the Japanese are out there.' By this time the peacock had gone, but it turned out there was a tiger just ahead of us. Tigers will sit for hours looking at a peacock, entranced with the colours."

Colonel Osborn and his troops formed a successful partnership with the Karen. "Clearly the news got round in the jungle that there were a whole lot of English soldiers advancing south, and so very quickly we received more and more information from the Karen," recalled Colonel Osborn. "We didn't cover more than 300 miles but as a result we eventually tracked down a complete Japanese corps of 30,000 men."

The Karens' loyalty was due to a number of factors. In Colonel Osborn's view, "They could see the protection from their enemies and they felt that no way could they progress if the Burmans got into power." The Karens could foresee, he added, what would happen to them if the Burmans were left in charge. "I also think they honestly really trusted us. People forget that in the British Empire, despites its mistakes, by and large the way we operated and the way religion played a big part in our life, appealed to them straight away." In addition, the British explorer mentality attracted them. "We were a people that could mix easily. It wasn't all about treading them underfoot. The British Empire would never have done so well for so long if that was the case. The spirit of adventure which is part of our nature appealed to the Karen."

Major Abbey believes the Karens' friendship with the British was "partly because of their nature, and partly because they were converted to Christianity and they felt an affinity for us". In addition to their love of the British, however, the other side of the coin was their hatred of the Burmans. "They had reasons to hate the Burmans because the Burmans despised the Karen as being a backward hill race."

The bond between the British soldiers and their Karen allies led, unfortunately, to some rash promises. "General Wingate and senior British officers who had fought with him said that when the war was over, they would work for the Karen to help them gain their independence and a country of their own," claims Bo Mya.[25] Some British soldiers admit making such promises. "I realised that they had a deep regard for the British. They were openly saying that they hoped they could remain part of the British Empire when the war was finished," Colonel Osborn recalls. "Without a moment's thought I said 'Yes of course, of course.'"

Major Abbey stopped short of making any promises of independence. "I never promised that they would have their independence. But I did say that I would do my utmost to see that they got a fair deal. I didn't want to make a categorical promise – but I didn't think for a moment that we would let them down as we did."

Those British soldiers who promised the Karen independence did so because they were so touched by the Karens' allegiance to them. "They were naïve, and they were over-whelmed by the kindness, generosity and sacrifice of the Karens," said Major Abbey. "They believed no one could turn their back on such generosity. It was unbelievable that we could have behaved as we did."

How did Britain behave? In essence, the British Government sided with its enemy's erstwhile ally against its most loyal friends. Aung San formed the Burma Independence Army (BIA) to campaign for an end to colonial rule, and allied with the Japanese against the British for most of the Second World War. In 1944, when Japanese fortunes were changing and the British were starting to gain the upper hand, the BIA under Aung San switched sides and joined the British. The Viceroy of India, Lord Mountbatten, had already authorised a secret deal with the Burmans before the end of the war, and the British then gave Aung San what he wanted, while distancing themselves from their most loyal allies, the Karen.

At the end of the war, a general election was held in Britain which the Conservative Party lost. Clement Attlee became Prime Minister of the new Labour Government, and immediately set about dismantling the British Empire. In Major Abbey's view, the speed with which this was done was wrong. "Independence had to happen but it was the way it was done. The Empire was not wicked. There were short-comings but it was not wicked. But I think the Attlee Government thought it was wicked and had to be got rid of," he said. In the case of Burma, however, "we were giving independence to the ambitious rulers, the politicians, and not to the ordinary people".

The British Government set to work negotiating a deal with Aung San. In November 1944, a group of young Conservative Members of Parliament had, in consultation with the exiled Governor of Burma Reginald Dorman-Smith, published a plan known as *The Blue Print for Burma*, advocating direct rule for a "reconstruction period" of up to six years. The paper also called for the formation of the Frontier Areas, including Kawthoolei, which "should not form part of the proposed Burmese dominion until such time as they clearly express a desire to join it".[26]

This was followed by a Government White Paper, in which Labour MPs had been involved, defining how this would work in practice.[27] It advocated keeping British Government control over the Frontier Areas "until such time as their inhabitants signify their desire for some suitable form of amalgamation with Burma proper".[28]

However, the attitude of the British Government changed towards the end of the war. In September 1945, the Karens drew up a memorandum proposing the creation of a "United Frontier Karen State", but the British Government did not respond. The Karens modified their proposal two months later with the suggestion that federal union with Burma was their ultimate goal. London still failed to respond.

Some British officials foresaw the possibility of a Karen uprising and tried to seek a solution. H.N.C. Stevenson, director of the Frontier Areas Authority, proposed holding a census of the Karen population and then forming a Karen territory within the Frontier Areas. He was criticised by the British and the Burmans and his ideas dismissed. At the end of 1946 he resigned. A few months later he warned London again of the serious consequences of ignoring the Karen: "At the time I left Burma the Karens were I believe under the impression that something was being done for them in London . . . I feel it is necessary that it should be made abundantly clear to them that all action rests with them and that nothing is being or can be done by London."[29]

However, events took over and the BIA were impatient for independence. So on 20th December, 1947, Attlee announced to the House of Commons that he was inviting Aung San and a Burmese delegation to London to discuss the transfer of power and, on 9th January, the delegation arrived. On 27th January, the "Attlee-Aung San Agreement" was signed granting Burma independence "as soon as possible". A general election would be held to establish a constituent assembly to draw up a constitution, and in the meantime an Executive Council (EC) – which included two Karens, one of whom was Saw Ba U Gyi – would act as the interim government.[30] But it should be noted that Aung San's delegation did not include any ethnic minority representatives. In Martin Smith's words, "The two Karen representatives on the EC were simply not invited."[31]

Attlee's Government refused to hear the appeals from the Karens and the other ethnic groups for autonomy or independence. The declared objective of both Britain and the new Burmese administration was "the early unification" of the different states of Burma. However, the Government did commit to achieving this aim "with the free consent of the inhabitants" of the "Frontier Areas". For that reason, all restrictions on Burmans in the Frontier Areas would be lifted, a conference would be held at Panglong to establish the views of the people in the Frontier Areas, and a Frontier Areas Committee of Enquiry (FACE) was established to take evidence of the wishes of the people in the Frontier Areas.[32]

But the British and Burmans never took account of the wishes of the people in the Frontier Areas. In August 1946, Saw Sydney Loo Nee led a delegation to Britain representing the Daw K'lu Association.[33] It became known as the "Goodwill Mission", and it included trained lawyers such as Saw Ba U Gyi, Saw Tha Din and Saw Po Chit.[34] But they met with blank faces and no sympathy for their separatist cause. The Karens wanted the Karen Hills and the Delta area for themselves in an autonomous self-governing system, but London ignored their requests.

Bo Mya, among many Karen, told of his disappointment.

"We wanted an independent country. We asked for it. We sent our leaders to Britain and petitioned for our independence, but they refused to give it to us. Instead they granted independence to the Burmese. If the British had divided the country, it would have ended there. They betrayed us."[35]

Many believe that despite his ardent nationalism, Aung San was nevertheless the best hope the Karens had. It was Aung San, after all, who convened the second Panglong Conference on 6th February, 1947, attended by the Shans, Kachins and Chins. The Karen and Karenni did not participate, although the Karen sent four observers. Six days later, the Panglong Agreement was signed, establishing the principle of the Union of Burma and enshrining the right of autonomy. Clause Five of the Panglong Agreement guaranteed that: "Full autonomy in internal administration for the Frontier Areas is accepted in principle."[36] Aung San sought to reassure the ethnic nationalities about his commitment to equality for all. He told them: "If Burma receives one kyat, you will also get one kyat."[37]

The Karens' attendance as observers, not participants, was a strategic mistake. They also boycotted the Governor's Executive Council and the Constituent Assembly elections – the bodies which were to draw up Burma's new Constitution. This had the disastrous result that the 1947 Constitution left out any reference to a Karen State and the entire question of the Karens' future was left to be decided after independence. It was proposed that if an agreement could not be reached after independence, a Karen State could be created out of lands in the Salween district, Karenni State and nearby Karen-majority areas, but without the right of secession granted to the Shan and Karenni. Indeed, the right of secession was expressly ruled out. Instead the Karen would be granted a Karen Affairs Council, a minister responsible for Karen issues and 22 seats in the Chamber of Deputies.[38] This was a long way from autonomy or independence.

As Aung San and others prepared for the Panglong confer-ence, the Karen held their own All Karen Congress and agreed to combine all their organisations and parties into a Karen Nation Union (KNU). They passed resolutions calling for a separate Karen State stretching as far as the coast.

Shelby Tucker argues that none of Burma's independence leaders "was more sympathetic to Karen aspirations than Aung San".[39] "While he stopped short of conceding their desire for full independence, he favoured a broad measure of regional autonomy and constitutional safeguards for ethnic rights and was at odds with colleagues precisely because he rejected Burman hegemony," writes Tucker. On 17th June, 1947 Aung San delivered a speech in which he said that "Burma should consist of specified Autonomous States . . . with adequate safeguards for minorities."[40]

Some, however, are not convinced. Major Abbey doubts that Aung San was sympathetic to the ethnic nationalities. "To hand it over to a man like Aung San was short-sighted, criminal, foolish to the extreme," said Major Abbey. "His pre-vious history was of just jumping from one side to the other, joining whoever could give him the best opportunity. He was determined to have independence for Burma."

We will never know the truth about Aung San's intentions because at half past ten in the morning on 19th July, 1947, four men burst into a cabinet meeting and assassinated Aung San and six of his ministers. It has been suggested that General Ne Win, who was later to become the leader of Burma, mas-terminded the murder.[41]

With Aung San dead, the prospects for the Karen and other ethnic nationalities looked even bleaker than ever. The new Prime Minister, U Nu, who presided over the final transfer of power from Britain to Burma and the birth of the new inde-pendent nation, stated: "I am a hundred [lit: cent] per cent against the creation of Autonomous States for the Karens,

Mons and Arakanese."[42] That signalled the direction relations between the ethnic groups and the Burmans would take for years to come.

Like many former soldiers, Colonel Osborn is disappointed with the way the Karen have been treated. "The Karen were people that we would have been proud to have had in the Empire. They were people worth helping not only in terms of humanity but because they were intrinsically a very nice, well-behaved, well-disciplined people," he says. "It seems to me that of all the people that need help in the world, the Karen come pretty high up on the list. I sometimes wonder whether perhaps charity is focused in the wrong direction. They really are worthy of much more attention than they get. If they disappear, the world will be poorer."

Major Abbey agrees. "Imagine how I and many others felt when the British Government supported Aung San and the Burmans, who had been actively against us, and completely failed to recognise the needs of the Karens, the Kachins, the Shans and the others."

The Burmans lost no time in crushing the Karen. On Christmas Eve 1948, Karen church congregations were slaughtered. As if abandoning the Karen were not bad enough, Attlee approved the shipment of arms to the Burmans to use to crush any Karen uprising.

Some of the British soldiers who had worked with the Karen were so outraged by the British Government's betrayal of their friends that they set to work assisting the Karen militarily. According to Alex Campbell, even before the deal had been finalised, the British forces in Burma had captured a significant amount of arms from the Japanese and because they already had doubts about Britain's policy, they gave the arms to the Karen in case they needed them to defend themselves. Although the British authorities tried to disarm the Karen, in 1949 those Karen who were not yet disarmed rose up, and other hill tribes followed. The civil war, which continues to this day, had begun.

A handful of British soldiers did not want to leave things as they were. Led by Lieutenant-Colonel Cromarty-Tulloch and backed by the former head of SOE, Major-General Colin Gubbins, and a former British Governor of Burma, and including the Editor of the *Daily Mail* Frank Owen, they formed the "Friends of the Burma Hill People". Lieutenant-Colonel Tulloch helped to direct operations from India, while Campbell worked in Burma with the Karen resistance. But such was Britain's determination to support Burma's independence and abandon the Karen that these Karen sympathisers soon came under MI5 surveillance. After Campbell arrived in Rangoon in 1948, the British Ambassador Sir James Bowker telegraphed the Foreign and Commonwealth Office:

> Campbell . . . has hinted that he is here for other purposes than mere journalism and that . . . he is backed by Owen and the *Daily Mail* to the tune of several thousand pounds. Campbell was in Karenni during the war as a member of Force 136. He is an old friend of Tulloch's and pays more frequent visits to Calcutta than would normally be justified by his work as a correspondent.[43]

Campbell was arrested in Burma after a request for arms, sent to Tulloch, was intercepted by intelligence services. He was jailed and sentenced to death, but then extradited. Owen was forced to resign as Editor of the *Daily Mail*, after the newspaper's owner Lord Rothermere found a Karen flag flying at the *Daily Mail*'s offices,[44] and Campbell and Tulloch agreed never to return to Burma. Attlee's Government, more even than the Burmese authorities, succeeded in crushing the plot to assist the Karen.

In a debate in the House of Commons on 5th November, 1947, Leader of the Opposition Winston Churchill disassociated himself from Attlee's deal. Referring to the Karen and other ethnic groups, Churchill told Parliament: "All loyalties have been discarded and rebuffed; all faithful service has been forgotten and brushed aside . . . We stand on the threshold of another scene of misery and ruin." He added that the deal was one "which should ever haunt the consciences of the principal actors in this tragedy".

The British betrayal of the Karens was not only evident in the post-war scramble for independence. Ever since that time, British politicians have washed their hands of their former allies. In a letter on 24th December, 1981 from the Lord Privy Seal and Foreign Office Minister Humphrey Atkins MP to John Page MP, which has never been published before, Britain's decision to abandon the Karen was made clear. At a time when gross violations of human rights were taking place, Mr Atkins wrote:

> Although it is certainly the case that the Burmese armed forces are engaged in continuous fighting with a variety of ethnic insurgent groups in the frontier areas, we have had no reports of anything approaching a civil war or of the Karens being subjected to genocide. I am well aware of the long history behind the Karens' claim to self-determination and of the very significant part they played in the colonial administration. Having said that, I do not believe there is anything we can usefully do to mediate between the Burmese Government and the Karens or any of the other ethnic minorities that are apt to collide with the Central Government. Even to try to do so would be seen inevitably as intervention in the internal affairs of another country.

A handwritten Foreign and Commonwealth Office briefing note on the Karen, written in 1982 and kept confidential until now, underlines the British Government's position:

> You ask whether there is any way we can help the Karen in view of their past loyalty to the British. The answer is no and, more-

over, we would not wish to do so. Whatever the historical background, we have no status nor interest in intervening in this civil war. If we did it would have disastrous consequences for our interests in Burma as a whole and in any event we have shed our imperial role and are no longer the world's policeman.

The author of this note failed to see any difference between the Karen resistance, struggling for survival, and the Burma Army, oppressing its people:

"Like in all civil wars . . . I have no doubt that unpleasant events take place. I have little doubt either that both sides are equally culpable in that respect."

The Prime Minister, Margaret Thatcher, who had been so strong in standing up to the tyranny of the Soviet Union, had little interest in the Karen or Karenni cause either. In a letter to Cyril Townsend MP on 27th March, 1986, she wrote:

The Karenni could be in no doubt of the British Government's position at the time of the negotiations. Earl Listowel, the Secretary of State for Burma, paid tribute to the Karen and by extension the Karenni, but warned: ". . . Once the transfer of power takes place there can no longer be any question of any interference by His Majesty's Government in the affairs of what will then be a sovereign state . . ." This remains the position.

Since then Britain's rhetoric became much more critical of Burma. However, it could have done, and could still do, much more to help its erstwhile allies.

The Karens' cause was not helped by the attitude of some British academics. Professor Hugh Tinker, author of a book called *The Union of Burma* and a lecturer at the University of Lancaster, wrote to Tony Stonor in 1982 arguing that the Karens' demands for autonomy were unreasonable, that they asked for too much land in 1947 and therefore blew their chances of any fair deal, and that they were wrong to boycott the 1947 elections. While it may be true that the Karen were over-ambitious in asking for Delta land, where they were in a minority, to be included in a Karen State, Professor Tinker's next point is remarkably naïve: "The regime in Burma is not the oppressive dictatorship you believe it to be," he wrote. "I believe there is more freedom in Burma than in India."

He blamed the British soldiers for giving the Karen false hope. Force 136 were, he claimed, "false friends" who "made the most extravagant promises to the Salween Karens to induce them to rise . . . None of these promises were cleared with their political masters in London or even with the Government of Burma." Unfortunately, he continued, "The Karens took all the promises as kosher. When they tried to cash the cheque, of course it bounced."

Remarkably, although the Karens' trust in the British may be dented, it is not destroyed. "We still have faith in the British," said Saw Kya Sein, a former Karen soldier. "We pray to Almighty God that He will touch their hearts. The people we are fighting do not believe in our God. We believe one day God will send the British back to help us. We firmly believe that."[45]

In 1946, Saw Yone Hla of the Amherst Karen Association, wrote to Major Abbey:

"England is so dear to the Karens and the Karens will remain loyal to the British Crown forever. You had lived with them, eaten with them, served with them, slept with them, played with them, fought with them, sang with them, ran with them, prayed with them, suffered with them."

The younger generation of Karens today do not share this loyalty to Britain. They have grown up in a different era, and feel little attachment to their nation's former colonial rulers. And some of the older generation who had been loyal question their own wisdom. Micah Rollings, for example, is frank about how he feels. For over half a century his people have been struggling for freedom. Thousands have been raped and killed. He is in no doubt where, ultimately, a large part of the responsibility lies. If Britain had sought to arbitrate a better deal for the ethnic groups, many lives may have been saved. "It is the betrayal of the British that is causing this suffering," he concluded. Some British politicians know this. "The British Government has repeatedly betrayed our former wartime allies, the Karen people," Lord Alton told the House of Lords in 1998. "Now is the time to make amends."

NOTES

1 Sometimes spelled Mika Rolly or Micah Rolley
2 Donald Mackenzie Smeaton, *The Loyal Karens of Burma*, p. 1
3 Ibid., p. 6
4 Dr San C Po, *Burma and the Karens*, p. 38
5 Harry Ignatius Marshall, *The Karen People of Burma*, p. 306
6 Ibid., p. 306
7 Ibid., p. 306
8 Ibid., p. 314
9 BBC Timewatch, *Forgotten Allies*
10 Lisa Chittabuck, *Britain's Betrayal: Genocide in Burma – Britain's betrayal of her World War II allies in Burma*
11 BBC
12 M.R.D. Foot, *The SOE in France*, p. 6
13 Ibid., p. 8
14 BBC
15 Ian Morrison, *Grandfather Longlegs: The Life and Gallant Death of Major H.P. Seagrim*, p. 78
16 Ibid., p. 81
17 James Mawdsley, *The Heart Must Break: The Fight for Democracy and Truth in Burma*
18 Morrison, p. 151

19 BBC
20 Ibid.
21 Hamilton Walters, *Introduction to the Tham Hin Historical Research Project*
22 Dr San C Po, p. 81
23 Ibid., p. 80
24 Ibid., p. 73
25 BBC
26 Martin Smith, *Burma, Insurgency and the Politics of Ethnicity*, p. 65
27 Shelby Tucker, *Burma: The Curse of Independence*, p. 106
28 Smith, p. 65
29 Ibid., p. 77
30 Tucker, pp. 118–120
31 Smith, p. 78
32 Tucker, p. 120
33 *Karen Heritage*, Issue 1, Volume 1, November 2002
34 Smith, p. 72
35 BBC
36 Smith, p. 78
37 Ibid., p. 78
38 Ibid., p. 82
39 Tucker, p. 151
40 Ibid., p. 152
41 Ibid., pp. 155–157
42 Ibid., p. 152
43 "Why Briton faced Briton in Burma", *Daily Telegraph*, 1997
44 Ibid.
45 BBC

CHAPTER THREE

"GIVE ME LIBERTY OR DEATH"

"For our struggle is not against flesh and blood,
but against the rulers, against the authorities, against the
powers
of this dark world and against the spiritual forces of
evil in the heavenly realms."
Ephesians 6:12

The soldiers lined up, their heads bowed. They were young men in their late teens, caught up in a struggle for survival. While boys their age in other countries were perhaps preparing for university or starting a job, these men were preparing to sacrifice their lives for their people. And their people have been fighting this struggle for over half a century.

Each one had an M16 slung over his shoulder, and a hand grenade on his belt. But many of them also carried a Bible in their pockets and a gentle smile on their faces. They were new recruits, completing basic training at a base just inside Burma. Crossing the river from Thailand, the first indication one has of being in another country is a little wooden sign with the words: "Welcome to Kawthoolei". Next to that, beside a guard post, is another sign which reads: "Give me liberty or death". Hanging on a wall in a bamboo hut near the parade ground are Saw Ba U Gyi's "Four Principles of the Karen Revolution":

There shall be no surrender.
The recognition of the Karen State must be completed.
We shall retain our own arms.
We shall decide our own political destiny.

These soldiers were part of the Karen National Liberation
Army (KNLA)'s effort to defend their people. As I looked at
them, I wondered how many would still be there in a few
months' time.

I read Psalm 91 to the soldiers, in the hope that it might
encourage them and equip them spiritually for the battles
ahead. The words seemed eerily appropriate:

He who dwells in the shelter of the Most High
will rest in the shadow of the Almighty.
I will say of the Lord, "He is my refuge and my fortress,
My God, in whom I trust."
Surely he will save you from the fowler's snare
And from the deadly pestilence.
He will cover you with his feathers,
And under his wings you will find refuge;
His faithfulness will be your shield and rampart,
You will not fear the terror of night,
Nor the arrow that flies by day,
Nor the pestilence that stalks in the darkness,
Nor the plague that destroys at midday.
A thousand may fall at your side,
Ten thousand at your right hand,
But it will not come near you.
You will only observe with your eyes
And see the punishment of the wicked.
If you make the Most High your dwelling –
Even the Lord, who is my refuge –
Then no harm will befall you,
No disaster will come near your tent.
For he will command his angels concerning you

To guard you in all your ways;
They will lift you up in their hands,
So that you will not strike your foot against a stone.
You will tread upon the lion and the cobra;
You will trample the great lion and the serpent.
"Because he loves me," says the Lord, "I will rescue him;
I will protect him, for he acknowledges my name.
He will call upon me, and I will answer him;
I will be with him in trouble,
I will deliver him and honour him.
With long life will I satisfy him
And show him my salvation.

Then Pastor Timothy, a Karen pastor who lives in exile from his homeland but works to promote his people's cause, spoke to the soldiers. He handed out Bibles to those who did not have them but wanted them. He spoke of his dismay at the international community's lack of interest in the Karen cause. "We cannot rely on men, on nations, on the United Nations," said Pastor Timothy. But then, a moment of hope in the midst of despair. "But with God, all things are possible." Holding up a Bible, he said "Only this book will deliver freedom and will bless our people."

Pastor Timothy invited any soldier who did not yet know the Lord, but who wanted to commit his life to Him, to come forward. Eleven young men came up. I was asked to pray for them. It was the first time I had ever prayed for someone with an M16 on their back and a hand grenade on their belt, but I knew that these men were fighting for truth and righteousness, as well as basic survival, so I had no fear. I just hoped that the Holy Spirit would not empower the gun and hand grenade immediately. Three were then baptised in the river.

Such an experience illustrates the blend of emotions and perspectives typical of the Karen people. Colonel Nerdah Mya, son of the former Karen National Union (KNU)

President General Bo Mya and a commander of the KNLA's Battalion 201, looked at me with a smile and said: "We fight with love, not with hatred. We fight simply to defend our people."

The Karens have been fighting this armed struggle since 1949. While the scene was being set for armed struggle throughout the negotiations for Burma's independence from 1945 onwards, it was the attacks on the Karen quarters in Rangoon on 30th January, 1949 that sparked the uprising. Just a few weeks before, on Christmas Eve 1948, local Burman militias known as *Sitwundans* threw hand grenades into the church at Palaw, Mergui district, killing 80 Christians who were celebrating the birth of Christ. A further 200 Karens were killed in nearby villages. Throughout January 1949 further, unprovoked attacks took place killing hundreds of Karens. The Karen National Defence Organisation (KNDO), which was formed in July 1947 and was banned in February 1949, raided the treasury at Maubin in the Lower Delta, in retaliation. The 4th Burma Rifles, led by General Ne Win, burned down the American Baptist Mission school in response. On 30th January, *Sitwundans* bombarded the Karen quarters at Thamaing and Ahlone in Rangoon with mortars and machine-gun fire, and destroyed dozens of homes.[1] Fighting began on the streets of Insein, and the Karen armed struggle was underway.

Louisa Benson Craig, daughter of Saw Benson, a Portuguese Jew who converted to Christianity and married a Karen, recalls the conflict in Insein. "We had a house up on the hill. Mr McSimon, my father's personal secretary, lived next door. We had a 60 acre property," she said. "Every night mortars were going off all over. During the daytime it seemed normal, but at night the shooting started. We had to stay away from the windows, and lie down on the floor to avoid being hit." One night Mr McSimon went out to close the gate, and was hit by shrapnel. "His cheek was gouged out and some shrapnel hit him in the knee. My father rushed out and took him to hospital."

Saw Benson was a wealthy man, who owned ice factories, mineral factories and 150 trucks. During this conflict he moved his family to the jungle near Bilin. But before they left Insein, Louisa witnessed terrible atrocities carried out by the Burmans. "They raped Karen girls. One girl was raped, her breasts were cut off, and she was hung to die. A Karen leader was made to watch as the Burmans raped his pregnant wife, then slit open her stomach and killed her. Then they killed him." The Burmans then headed for Bilin – but fortunately Louisa and her mother were already on their way back to Rangoon when the assault on Bilin began.

The Karen are, as those British soldiers who worked with them in the Second World War said, excellent soldiers, and they now had the experience of several years of war against the Japanese. Their struggle started off well, with the temporary capture of significant towns such as Henzada, Mandalay and Toungoo just three months after the civil war began.

But while the armed conflict began in earnest in 1949, the seeds of the struggle had been sown for many years. The Karens' support for the British in the Anglo-Burmese wars in the nineteenth century, and in suppressing the Saya San rebellion of 1930–32, had provoked grievous retaliation from the Burmans. Then towards the end of the Second World War, the Burma Independence Army (BIA), which had sided with the Japanese for most of the war, launched attacks against Karen villages. In Papun district in the eastern hills, several Karen elders were executed, and in Myangmya district it was reported that over 1,800 Karens were killed and 400 villages destroyed.[2] The Karen leader Saw Pe Tha, who had served in the colonial Cabinet before the war, was assassinated, along with 152 other Karens. In light of this, Karen leader Saw Tha

Din asked: "How could anyone expect the Karen people to trust the Burmans after what happened during the war – the murder and slaughter of so many Karen people and the robbing of so many Karen villages? After all this, how could anyone seriously expect us to trust any Burman government in Rangoon?"[3]

And there lay the problem. The wounds of history were too deep for the Karen to consider being ruled by the Burmans. After independence, in an attempt to mollify the Karen, the Burmese Government appointed two Karen officers to the top positions in the armed forces. General Smith Dun became commander-in-chief of the Burma Army, and Saw Shi Sho took the post of Air Force chief. This helped to secure the loyalty of those Karens serving in the Burma Army. But ultimately it was a token gesture and the two men were removed from their positions in January 1949.

In 1948 Saw Ba U Gyi wrote to U Nu repeating the KNU's demand for Karen territory in the Delta region. This was followed by a mass protest by over 400,000 Karens who took to the streets in towns all around the country, carrying banners with four clear demands:

Give the Karen State at once – Independence;
For the Burmese one kyat and the Karen one kyat – Equality;
We do not want communal strife – National Unity;
We do not want civil war – Peace.[4]

U Nu offered to meet with Saw Ba U Gyi and the KNU, but the talks simply underlined the chasm that existed between them. U Nu believed that the Karen State was already provided for in the Constitution, and demanded that the Karen enter the Parliament and participate in the political process if they wanted to amend the Constitution. Saw Ba U Gyi knew, however, that the Karens would not have enough representation in the Parliament to stand a chance of making their desired amendments. However, despite the failure of these talks, the two men remained in close contact with each other and did their best to avert a violent uprising. They toured the Lower Delta region together and, surprisingly given how events developed, Saw Ba U Gyi publicly promised that the KNU would never resort to force.

Soon after the armed struggle had begun, the long-awaited Regional Autonomy Enquiry Commission started its work. It was a much more representative body than its predecessor, the Frontier Areas Commission of Enquiry (FACE), and included six Karens, led by Saw Ba U Gyi. But the conclusions were just as unsatisfactory for the Karens. While the Karens repeated their desire for independence, they also refused to rule out the possibility of being part of a federal union. The Karens even proposed a joint Karen–Mon State given the alliance that had developed between the two ethnic groups after the Karen capture of Moulmein. However, the Commission's recommendations did not meet the Karen demands – the geographical area proposed, and the requirement that the Karen State be part of the Union, were not acceptable to the Karen leadership.

With the hope of a political solution acceptable to all sides becoming ever more remote, the Karens' armed struggle gathered pace. In January 1949 Karen forces came within four miles of Rangoon. They held out in Insein, nine miles from Rangoon, in a 112-day siege which was only broken through the mediation of the British and Commonwealth ambassadors and Bishop West, a man well-respected by the Karen Christians. However, U Nu and General Ne Win refused to accept a general ceasefire and fighting began again on 9th April, 1949. On 20th May, the Karen declared the formation of the Karen State from their capital at Toungoo, and Saw Ba U Gyi was appointed as the first prime minister. A year later the KNU moved the capital to Papun.

On 12th August, 1950, the KNU suffered its first major setback. Saw Ba U Gyi, the man who had given the Karen cause clear leadership, was ambushed along with Saw Sankey, and murdered. His body is believed to have been taken to Moulmein by the Burma Army, displayed in public, and then dumped into the sea. The Burma Army not only assassinated the Karen leader, but also denied the Karens the opportunity of burying him in Kawthoolei.

Saw Ba U Gyi is widely revered by the Karen as the father of their struggle. His daughter, Thelma Gyi-Baerlein, describes him as a man who "loved life". The son of a wealthy landowner, Tha Mya Kyi, Saw Ba U Gyi was educated at Magdalen College, Cambridge, and then qualified as a barrister at Middle Temple, London, in 1929. He learned not only English but also Latin, and married an English woman. The couple had two children, and his wife learned Sgaw Karen and became involved with Karen women's organisations and Karen Girl Guide groups.

"He was good looking with the most natural ease and good taste. He made friends and mixed with his entourage regardless of position, race or culture," his daughter recalls. However, he was a fierce Karen nationalist. "I have to confess that I don't remember father bringing a Burman into our home," she adds.

Brought up in a Baptist family, Saw Ba U Gyi's Christian faith was central to his approach to life. "He believed in God and he worshipped him. He believed in doing unto others as you would others do unto you," his daughter said. "The Christian faith and the way of living influenced his outlook and actions, as it does all Karen Christians. Christianity was his foundation. His education as a barrister was built on that foundation. Those two factors coupled with his character made him the leader that he was."

The former British Governor, Sir Reginald Dorman-Smith, was one of those who admired Saw Ba U Gyi. He wrote to *The Times* after his death:

"Saw Ba U Gyi was no terrorist . . . I, for one, cannot picture him enjoying the miseries and hardships of a rebellion. There must have been some deep impelling reason for his continued resistance."[5]

The KNU was faced with the daunting challenge of identifying a new leader. Temporarily Skaw Ler Taw stepped into the breach, but Saw Hunter Tha Hmwe was chosen as the permanent successor to Saw Ba U Gyi.

After the murder of Saw Ba U Gyi, the Burma Army – and Burma's Government – achieved a second scalp with the assassination of Colonel Lin Htin in 1965. His widow Louisa Benson Craig, a former Miss Burma, still does not know exactly how he was killed, but believes he was drugged at a dinner at a friend's home and then shot. "He was very quick-witted and quick on the draw – he used to tell me not to worry about him being shot because he would be too quick for them. But of course if he had been drugged, they could then kill him easily," she argues.

Lin Htin was one of the best Karen soldiers. Robert Zan served with his infamous 5th Brigade forces and recalls their discipline. "When I was an operational commander and was with Lin Htin's troops, we were in the jungle on one occasion and I was very tired. I wanted to sleep," he recalls. "But Lin Htin's soldiers were told to build their huts first before they could sleep. He was very tough, but also kind, and a man who insisted on very good equipment and discipline."

Louisa Benson Craig acknowledges that her former husband had "a terrible reputation with women" but she "respected him as a patriot and a nationalist". The suggestion made by some historians that Lin Htin surrendered to the Burmese is nonsense, she argues.

He did, however, gain a reputation for being unpredictable. In 1960, for example, he launched an attack on the Thai town of Mae Sot, where much of the KNU is now based. Louisa

Benson Craig does not know exactly why Lin Htin attacked Mae Sot, but believes that he had struck an arms deal with a Thai businessman which fell through. "He had handed over the money for the arms, but the person did not deliver. That may have been why he attacked Mae Sot."

The assassinations of Saw Ba U Gyi in 1950 and Lin Htin in 1965 deprived the KNU of two of its greatest leaders. But the Karen cause was also damaged by growing splits in the 1950s and 1960s over political ideology. For a time the KNU sought to develop an alliance with the Communist Party of Burma (CPB). They learned the lesson of 1949, when the KNU and CPB went separate ways, largely because the CPB leader Than Tun viewed Saw Ba U Gyi as "a lackey of imperialism".[6] If they had united at that time, their combined forces could have led to the capture of Rangoon, but it was not to be.

Learning from the CPB's tactics, and even discussing military alliances with the CPB, were one thing, but in the mid-1950s, according to Martin Smith, the Karen leaders "embarked on a period of selective experimentation with communist ideology".[7] This led to the first major split in the KNU. The KNU President, Saw Hunter Tha Hmwe, disagreed profoundly with the KNU military strategist Mahn Ba Zan over developing a relationship with the CPB.[8]

When Saw Hunter Tha Hmwe parted company with Mahn Ba Zan, he asked Bo Mya, one of his senior commanders, to decide which side he would join. Bo Mya was anti-communist, but he told Tha Hmwe that he would need to talk to Mahn Ba Zan before making a decision. Mahn Ba Zan assured Bo Mya he was not a communist. He was a Christian, and a socialist. "I believe in God and I am praying every day," Mahn Ba Zan told Bo Mya. "If that is the case I will follow you. But if you are a communist, I'll depart from you," Bo Mya replied.[9]

Bo Mya returned to Saw Hunter Tha Hmwe and told him that Mahn Ba Zan denied being a communist, and for that reason he was going to follow him. "I know you are patriotic and a nationalist, but your subordinates are doing things I do not like – raping and killing people," Bo Mya told him. "Today I may not follow you. But one day, if I know you are going the right way, I may do so. But please do not go back and surrender to the Burmans." Saw Hunter Tha Hmwe told him he was simply going to go home and become a farmer.

Saw Hunter Tha Hmwe talked with the Burmese Government and asked for a Karen homeland. The Burmans lied to him. They announced on the radio that Karen State would be called Kawthoolei and the capital would be at Pa'an, but they lied. "They installed a governor – they did not give Kawthoolei to the Karen," said Bo Mya.

It was not long before Bo Mya began to regret his decision. He claims Mahn Ba Zan became increasingly "Red" and Karen villagers started to complain that the leadership was communist. "We are Christians. How can we worship God if we have a communist leadership?" they asked Bo Mya.

Bo Mya went straight to the KNU headquarters and told them they had to change their policy towards the Communists immediately. "We are not fighting for the Communists, for Mao Zedong, we are fighting for the Karen cause," he told them. "I said this three or four times. But they did not listen to me. They ignored what I said – so later I split from them."

In 1966, Bo Mya, a member of the Central Committee of the KNU, was joined by four other Central Committee members in leaving the KNU and forming the Karen National Liberation Council (KNLC), and its armed wing, the Karen National Liberation Army (KNLA). He became President of the KNLC and commander of the KNLA in 1965, and carried with him the Karens in eastern Karen State.

A year later, Mahn Ba Zan and others joined Bo Mya and, despite their differences, they attempted to reunite the Karen forces. But the power struggle between them continued.

Although he agreed to work with him again, Bo Mya still suspected that Mahn Ba Zan was a communist sympathiser. The final straw was when Ba Zan expressed the hope that China would support the ethnic resistance in Burma and said that in the struggle between the Burmese regime, the CPB and the ethnic nationalities, the KNU would side with whichever group accepted the essential components of the ethnic struggle. Bo Mya countered that statement with the announcement of a policy that the KNU would only accept help from capitalist nations, and in August 1976 Mahn Ba Zan agreed to stand down as President of the KNU and become an "honorary adviser". Bo Mya became President, Minister of Foreign Affairs and Minister of Defence, while maintaining his role as Chief of Staff of the KNLA all in one go,[10] thus securing a power base in the KNU which cemented his influence over the Karen struggle for the next three decades. He controlled a powerful armed force, and began to develop an anti-communist alliance with Thailand. The Communists were growing in Thailand, and so the Karen worked to prevent any alliance between the CPB and the Thai Communists.

Mahn Ba Zan's son Robert Zan refutes the allegation that his father was a communist. He admits that much of his military strategy was learned from the example of the CPB and the Communist revolution in China, but that, Zan claims, was because access to literature was limited. "After independence, all the books available came from the Communists," he says. "But he was not a communist. He studied communism, socialism, imperialism, and how independence could be achieved."

In fact, Mahn Ba Zan was a committed Christian, his son believes. "In his dying days he lost his sight, but he called me to his side and recited Psalm 23, Psalm 27 and Psalm 91. He told me not to forget them."

Bo Mya converted to Christianity from Animism through his marriage in 1962 to Thra Mu Lah Po, a Seventh Day

Adventist Karen, and under his leadership Christianity has been a dominant influence on the Karen struggle. In fact, Bo Mya enforced a draconian moral code with quasi-Old Testament penalties – people found guilty of adultery are imprisoned, alcohol is banned and the possession, consumption and dealing of drugs all carry the death penalty. Whether this comes from the zeal of a convert or the belief that sex, drink and drugs impede the armed resistance, or a combination of the two, is unclear but there is no doubt that Bo Mya has instilled much greater discipline into his forces. A pastor close to Bo Mya told me once that he would like to see a free Karen State develop as a "theocracy" rather than a "democracy". I suggested that if that was the case, he keep that opinion to himself when travelling the world to lobby for support for the Karen cause.

Although the discipline and morality that Bo Mya brought to the struggle have been positive in many respects, his leadership at times has also shown little regard for the values of democracy and human rights for which the Karens are fighting. Anyone who disobeys or disregards Bo Mya's instructions does so at a price. Saw Lincoln Ja, for example, wished to establish the first college in the Karen resistance-controlled area. As a teacher, he was already giving classes in English, history, geography and agriculture to Karen high school students. But although local KNU education officials supported his plan, their superiors rejected it. Saw Lincoln went ahead anyway – and ended up in custody. Bo Mya placed him under house arrest for seven years for insubordination. When Saw Lincoln appeared before the General to present his case, and spoke directly to him, Bo Mya, known for his hot temper, was furious. "He was so mad that he was slapping the walls," Saw Lincoln said.[11]

While the internal power struggles and splits among the Karen were taking place, there were changes in Burma's political landscape too. In 1958, U Nu was persuaded by the military chief General Ne Win to hand over power to him temporarily, under the guise of restoring order and ending the civil war. Martin Smith describes this as "a military coup by any other name".[12] Others, such as Louisa Benson, who was in Burma at the time, believe U Nu genuinely expected to resume control after the caretaker military government had quelled the violence. Indeed, in 1960 an election was held, which U Nu won, but that was to be the last democratic election in Burma for 30 years. Two years after U Nu was returned to government, Ne Win staged a military coup, signalling the death knell of democracy in Burma.

Harn Yawnghwe, son of Burma's first President Sao Shwe Thaike, a Shan prince, recalls the coup. "The military surrounded our house and opened fire for about an hour," he said. "Our house was the only place they did that – right in the middle of Rangoon." Sao Shwe Thaike was arrested and imprisoned, and died eight months later, in jail. He had been President when U Nu was first Prime Minister and was widely perceived as the only man who could unite the ethnic nationalities in Burma and hold the country together. "They said it was a bloodless coup but actually my older brother was killed," said Harn Yawnghwe.

Harn and remaining family decided to flee the country. Despite being a wealthy family, they left with only the clothes on their backs. "We left everything. My father was very patriotic and since it was illegal to take money out of the country, we left it all. We knew that the military would confiscate our property – we owned lots of rice paddy fields – so we decided to give it all away." The family sought refuge initially in Thailand, and then in Canada.

With U Nu and Sao Shwe Thaike in jail, and a new military hardman at the helm, the prospect of a fair political solution for the Karen looked bleak. Ne Win tore up the 1947

Constitution, and began to close Burma down. The Ford, Fullbright and Asia Foundations were expelled, the teaching of English was curtailed, foreign journalists and missionaries banned, and businesses, mission schools and hospitals were nationalised. Democracy activist Ko Aung recalls that his mother lost three businesses: in 1962 the Government took all her family's land in Shan State, in 1964 they confiscated her tea export business, and in 1967 her rice export company was nationalised. She was one of many to suffer the economic consequences of Ne Win's policies.

On 7th July, 1962 troops were sent in to crack down on protesting students – and it would not be the last time. Ne Win rejected federalism, and imposed restrictions on Christians. The distribution of the Bible, for example, was restricted and pastors were urged not to preach on certain parts of the Old Testament which were seen to incite rebellion.[13]

And so the armed struggle continued. It attracted new recruits, including women like Mary On. Born in 1933, she grew up as a revolutionary. Her father joined the Karen resistance from the beginning, and when she completed her high school studies in 1951 he told her as he lay dying with malaria that it was now her turn to do something for Kawthoolei.

Mary On decided to take up her father's challenge. But rather than become a nurse or a teacher for the resistance, she wanted to take up arms herself. She became only the second woman soldier in the Karen resistance, although it took some effort on her part to convince the KNLA to allow her to fight. Initially she approached a colonel in the KNLA and told him she wanted to be a soldier. He set her a test he thought she could never pass. He told her to go to Rangoon and beg or steal a revolver.

The journey to Rangoon was a long, hard and dangerous one but Mary was determined to prove that she could be a soldier. She succeeded. Obtaining a gun in Rangoon, she bandaged it to her leg underneath a sarong, and made the trek home. Part of the journey was by steamer down the river, and on the boat she met her former headmistress, a Karen who was returning from the United States to Bassein. She hid the gun underneath her headmistress' pillow in her first class cabin.

When Mary arrived back at her village, she went straight to the Colonel.

"Where is the gun?" he asked.

"Here," she replied, pointing to her leg.

"You're bluffing," he replied.

She handed him the revolver, and he was astonished. As a reward, he offered her a wristwatch. Defiantly, she refused it. "I do not want to watch. I want to be a soldier. I want a gun," she said.

The Colonel gave her a gun, but when her uncle saw it he told her it was useless. It would hardly work. "I think they thought a woman would just shoot everything," she recalls.

Finally, Mary On got her gun – a decent rifle – and she began to be sent on undercover missions. She fought in the trenches, but she would also sneak behind the enemy lines to gather information.

"I would disguise myself sometimes as a pregnant woman, or an old man, or a little girl," she explains. "On one occasion I was dressed as a little boy with a sling bag. A Burmese soldier saw me and said: 'Hey, little boy, where are you going?' With my sarong around my face, I answered him: 'I am finding my buffalo.' On another occasion I dressed as an old woman, and my face looked like old Mother Hubbard. I went into villages and towns in Burma and as I went, I prayed to God to give me different faces. I was never discovered, and I was able to bring reports out to our soldiers."

Mary started to work with Bo Mya, and initially he thought she would not last long. "He said I would marry soon. But I told him I am not like the others. My troops are my brothers and I would sacrifice myself for my people," she said. For as long as she was able to serve the resistance, that was what she would do. "I told him that I would only walk down the aisle with a walking stick!"

In one battle, fifteen Karen soldiers, led by Major Luther, were on an island besieged by the Burma Army in boats and steamers, and Bo Mya asked some of his men to go to help. He dispatched Mary to Rangoon, Mopotaw and then to the island. She travelled at night, this time disguised as a rice farmer. Her hands were dirty and she pretended to be illiterate. Someone stopped her and asked if she could read. When she said she could not, they gave her a newspaper as a test. She held it upside down, and they were convinced.

Miraculously, Mary arrived at the island at night and helped the Karen soldiers escape. They got into three boats. "We almost gave ourselves away because each time the rower rowed, a little bell on the boat rang – 'cling cling' – very loud. My heart trembled like hell. But, by a miracle, the Burmese did not hear us," she explains.

They sailed down the river and across the Tongtay Canal. "One night as we were going down the canal, a Burmese came with a big torch and stopped us. 'Where are you going?' he asked. 'We're going to Rangoon for Farmer's Day,' I told him in a little voice. Miraculously, they left us alone."

Major Mary On is an experienced soldier and intelligence officer, but she also uses her female characteristics to help the resistance. She used to run through the battle lines taking fruit, fish paste, gourdes, and other food to the soldiers on the frontline. She is also the Karens' very own Vera Lynn, singing a range of Karen revolutionary songs, interspersed with American Country and Western songs, and strumming on her guitar. As she sat in her bamboo hut in the refugee camp which is now her home, she sang this song which she composed herself:

Kawthoolei, a wonderous motherland,
Discovered by our forefathers' clan.
Harmonious land,
The Burmans grab from our hands,
Subjugate and oppress us since then.

Nowadays our Karen will never be your slaves
Till 'tis the time of grace.

Banners raised
With might and mare
Till the time of victory.

Nowadays our Karen will never give away
Fight without delay
Stormy weather
Survive or die
The land we crave for equal rights.

After the fall of the Karen headquarters at Manerplaw in 1995, she retired from frontline duty and became a refugee. But she continued to work for several years, as Chairman of the Karen Refugee Committee, before retiring completely a few years ago. Now, she says, "I am simply praying and meditating and reading the Bible." She longs to go home, but only when it is safe to do so. "If there is genuine peace today, we will go back tonight, we will not wait until tomorrow," she said. She urged Christians around the world to pray for the Karen, for "charity, unity and honesty". She does not hate the Burmans, but she hates the system. "We hate the system, a system which kills, plunders, loots and rapes. Before we go to hell or heaven, we must struggle. The Lord has given us a bitter cup to drink. But we must drink it. We must pray that the Lord will have mercy on us and shorten our suffering." There is, she added, only one hope. "We have to turn to God, not to the British, or the Burmese, or to fighting." One day "there will be a miracle", and the Karen will receive equal rights in Burma. "God is our freedom," she concluded.

Whether as soldiers in the jungle or refugees in Thailand, the Karen value education highly. Robert Zan, Mahn Ba Zan's son, joined the resistance in 1964 and fought for 33 years before moving to the United States. He became the Company Commander of Battalion 19 in the 7th Brigade. In the jungle, he used to take with him what he called a "mobile library", so that he could keep studying and learning. Some books were political, some were literature, and some related to military tactics. "Although there was basic military and officer training, there was no military academy," he said. "So I took with me manuals from the SAS, the US Special Forces, the Rangers, and books about Che Guevarra, the Vietnamese revolution, Mao Zedong and the Burma Army General Staff. I learned from books and from the battlefield."

Hope, the daughter of a Karen commander, is another person who values education – and her name is appropriate. The sacrifices she has made in order to pursue her schooling are impressive. Her family had no money for school, and so at the age of eleven, her father told her the only way she could continue her education was to go and work for a family in the 7th Brigade area, and save up the funds for school. She walked barefoot for three days and three nights, crossing through the heart of Tatmadaw-controlled territory, to get to her destination, and there, lonely and homesick, knowing nobody, she worked as a cleaner. Along the way, the Burma Army shelled the group of five she was travelling with, and two died. "My father had to bind my feet with cloth. We could not afford shoes," she said. "I had to clean the house, wash clothes, clean the toilet and look after a one-year-old baby, for one year. In return, the family I worked for said they would send me to school. At school I tried very hard, and at the end of my first year I came top of the class. My teachers gave me new clothes and found funds to support me for the rest of my school years."

But in addition to sheer hard work, Hope prayed hard and witnessed several miracles. In her final year at school she wanted to sit the exams. But for all nine subjects, she had to pay a total exam fee of 1,080 Thai Baht. "I only had 90 Baht. I asked if I could borrow money from my teachers, but they refused. I asked my auntie, but she could not help. So I prayed for a miracle," she said. "The day before the exams I woke up, unrolled my clothes – and there, to my surprise, was 300 Baht inside my pocket. It was not there before. Immediately I informed the camp leader because I did not want to be accused of being a thief. He told me to use it for the exam fee."

As a child, Hope's father was often in the front line, in the 6th Brigade area. One day, her mother found there was no more food left in the house to feed Hope, her three brothers and their aunt. Her husband would be gone a long time, and they had no rice and no money. The family prayed, and then the eldest son went out to pick bananas. To his surprise, he found five tins of rice in the jungle. "No one brought the rice. It was just there, on the ground. It was a miracle. And the next day, my father came home, bringing more rice," recalls Hope.

Some soldiers, however, start remarkably young with almost no education. While the Karen have a policy of discouraging child soldiers, and giving everyone up to the age of 18 the opportunity to go to school, there are children who volunteer for the KNLA. Unlike the Burma Army, however, which has forced over 70,000 child soldiers to join the military, the children in the KNLA are usually there by choice. More often than not they have seen relatives killed by the Burma Army, and decided to join the resistance as a result.

The most famous child soldiers among the Karen were the twins, Johnny and Luther Htoo, who formed what became known in the Western media as the "God's Army". Based on a strange mixture of Christianity, Buddhism and Animism, these children, aged just 12 years old at the time, were believed to possess spiritual powers to defeat the Burmese enemy. Never endorsed by the KNLA, God's Army was a breakaway group formed by soldiers who were tired of the lack of progress in the Karen struggle and inspired by the twins' mythical reputation.

The God's Army – or, as its name in Karen is more correctly translated, the "Soldiers of the Holy Mountain" – grew to a force of 200 at one stage. It began in 1997, in the village of Htaw Ma Pyo, when the Burma Army launched a major offensive to clear land for the construction of the Bongti highway and the completion of the Yadana gas pipeline, a joint venture between the French oil company Total, the US oil firm Unocal and the Burmese junta which provides the regime with $200–400 million a year. Over 100,000 Karen fled to Thailand and hundreds of thousands were displaced, taken for forced labour, or killed. The twins, aged eight at the time, claimed to have had a vision from God in which they had been commanded to lead their people against the Burma Army.

It was their extraordinary military success that gave rise to the myths about the twins' magical powers. They led a small group of soldiers in an attack against the Burma Army at the Aman Pass. According to one foreign observer who was in the area at the time, "the Burmese were eating dinner. It was about 6.30 p.m. They panicked and retreated all the way back to Tiki. That was the first God's Army victory."

Between 1997 and 1998, the God's Army fought an average of ten battles a week against the Burma Army. In one battle, they killed 23 Burmese soldiers without losing any of their own.[14] They developed a strange puritanical set of rules – no alcohol, no swearing, no womanising, but also no duck, pork or eggs.

The twins were looked after by their uncle, David, but Rambo the bodyguard provided security. Rambo was a Christian who wore his Bible round his neck in a green purse,[15] and his faith on his sleeve. One of Rambo's tasks was to translate Scriptures for Luther, who could not read. One of their favourite verses was from 1 Corinthians 1:27:

> But God chose the foolish things of the world to shame the wise; God chose the weak things of the world to shame the strong.

Another popular verse was 1 Timothy 6:12: "Fight the good fight of the faith. Take hold of the eternal life to which you were called . . ."[16]

God's Army was, however, ultimately a passing moment in the Karen armed struggle. Despite amazing successes, the supposedly supernatural powers of the twins were not enough to sustain a small band of men against more than 21,000 Burma Army soldiers in their area. And despite their mythical reputation, Johnny and Luther were, at the end of the day, children who ought to have been in school. In 2000 the two boys turned themselves in to the Thais, and were reunited with their mother in a refugee camp.

Mainstream Karen Christians dismiss God's Army as a cult. Some even believe it was a creation of the SPDC to divide the Karen. While God's Army had Christian values and based its beliefs on the Bible, it distorted orthodox Christian teaching and mixed it up with Animist beliefs. "It was founded with good intent, but it got corrupted," said one foreign missionary who met the twins in 1997.

Despite the spiritual distortions, God's Army certainly served as a symbol of hope and inspiration for the otherwise beleaguered Karen armed resistance – which had been held back by splits and divisions.

The Karens have been fighting their armed struggle for over

half a century. They are tired of war and they do not want to continue fighting, but they know that for their survival they have to defend their people. "How many lives have been destroyed during the fifty years of this civil war in Burma? How many tears have fallen for those who have died?" writes Robert Zan. "How much property has been destroyed? How many widows have been made? How many human bodies have been mutilated and disabled? There has been countless suffering over the last fifty years of civil war, so much suffering that only God can calculate it."[17]

Robert Zan describes his feelings towards the enemy, feelings typical of the forgiving, gracious character of the Karen. Recalling one ambush which he led against the Tatmadaw, he writes:

> At last the enemy came . . . In the moonlight I could see them clearly. With my finger on the trigger of my Browning Automatic Rifle, I tried to concentrate on the fire fight that was soon to come, but my mind was in conflict. On the one hand, I felt that the approaching enemy was responsible for my brother's death. They were the ones that burned our Karen villages and raped our Karen women. On the other hand, the enemy in front of me were young men who had not chosen to join the Burma Army but were forcibly conscripted. All of us had been born in the same country and we were all brothers. We did not know each other and we had no personal conflict with each other. I knew that soon they would be dying in front of me. I would be killing them. I felt both hatred and brotherly union spirit towards them.[18]

The Karens' fight, for some of them at least, is kept alive by two heartfelt beliefs: their passion for Kawthoolei combined with a zealous Christian faith. "I have been telling our soldiers this is our country, our land – someone else has invaded it," explained Colonel Nerdah Mya. "That is why we have to fight for our people. We cannot give up while the people are being oppressed and killed. We have to stand up for ourselves, for the needy, to protect the people. We have to fight for right-eousness and establish the truth, and then the truth will set us free."

That belief gives them hope. "The Burmese soldiers may be more than us, but if we put God in front of us we have more than them and we become a huge number," said Colonel Mya. "Before I go into battle I line up the soldiers and I pray for them. We will let God fight with us, and so that is how we have gained back some of our land. Nothing is impossible with God." In the Bible, he points out, there are plenty of stories of God leading people to freedom. "If you look at Genesis and Exodus, at the story of Moses for example, people were only freed when they were led by God. Freedom for the Karen people must come from God. Man cannot do it."

Ultimately, Colonel Mya believes the battle is a spiritual one. "This is not real fighting, it is shadow fighting," he said. "The real fighting is in the spiritual realms. The real enemy is here, in your heart. You have to overcome your mind before your enemy does. I tell the soldiers that they can win a battle but they can still lose the war if they don't know how to control their minds."

NOTES

1 Martin Smith, *Burma: Insurgency and the Politics of Ethnicity*, p. 118
2 Ibid., p. 62
3 Ibid., p. 62
4 Ibid., p. 110
5 Ibid., p. 144
6 Ibid., p. 149
7 Ibid., p. 170
8 General Bo Mya, interview with the author

9 Ibid.

10 Smith, p. 298

11 Hamilton Walters, *Introduction to the Tham Hin Historical Research Project*

12 Smith, p. 175

13 Ibid., p. 205

14 Maximilian Wechsler, *The Rise and Fall of God's Army*, Czech Press, November 15, 2000

15 Maggie O'Kane, "Two little boys", *The Guardian*, July 27, 2000

16 Ibid.

17 Robert Mahn Ba Zan, *War, Love, Loss . . . and Hope*, http:karenstruggle.20mcom/intro.html

18 Ibid.

CHAPTER FOUR

COMRADES IN ARMS

"In '88, the people see a chance to win democracy
They faced the guns courageously but thousands died so
bloodily
Many men went into jail, many women went into jail
The bravest one most certainly was Burma's own Aung San
Suu Kyi
The People love Aung San Suu Kyi who talked about
democracy
While facing guns courageously and went to prison so
willingly
Since '89 she has been jailed: like Mandela she must be
hailed!
Although she won the Nobel Prize, SLORC will jail her
until she dies.
Let's organise and spread the word: demonstrate around the
world!
Trying hard to set them free, dear Burma and Aung San Suu
Kyi.
We must stand up for human rights! We must march on for
freedom's fight!
With peace we want democracy! These thoughts are from
Aung San Suu Kyi."

By David Law, 1992
(based on the tune of *The Ballad of the Green Beret*)

Walking round the Buddhist monastery in Rangoon, an English tourist was admiring the golden architecture. A monk greeted him with a gentle smile, and a conversation began. Initially they talked about the philosophy of Buddhism. They talked about inner peace, and the beauty of Burma. And then the Englishman grew a bit bolder. He asked the monk what he thought of "The Lady".

Before he had even mentioned her name – Aung San Suu Kyi – within seconds four men in monk's robes flew out from the shadows like something from a Bruce Lee kung fu film. With karate chops to his head, stomach, knees and groin, the Englishman was felled, rolling around the floor in agony. He picked himself up, bloodied and bruised, and left before they could do any more damage.

This was Burma, a land where Buddhism is the state religion but also the state tool of oppression. Although Buddhism is a philosophy of peace, and many Buddhist monks have sacrificed much in standing up for democracy and justice in Burma, the regime cloaks itself in the language and imagery of Buddhism whilst practising brutal and violent oppression. It even resorts to having agents dressed as monks planted in monasteries, ready to lash out at any potential critics or opponents of the regime.

But it should be emphasised that it is the regime itself which uses Buddhism as a political tool, and not Buddhists per se who are the oppressors. Many Buddhists themselves are oppressed in Burma, if they belong to an ethnic group such as the Shan which is fighting the regime, or if they are active in the democracy movement. And whatever religious differences there might be between the different groups, there has been a growing realisation that the Burman democracy forces and the ethnic resistance need to come together to overthrow an evil and illegal regime.

Uniting all resistance groups, both armed and non-violent, is a belief in democracy and a profound respect and love of the

Burmese democracy movement's leader, Nobel Laureate Daw Aung San Suu Kyi. The daughter of Aung San, she is now seen as Burma's Nelson Mandela, the one who has the capacity, if anyone does, of uniting the peoples of Burma and building a free, democratic, just and peaceful society.

Aung San Suu Kyi's role in the struggle started in earnest in 1988. The previous year, Ne Win, who had become increasingly involved in occult activities and developed an intense attachment to astrology, infuriated the Burmese people by deciding, overnight, to demonetise much of the Burmese currency. His astrologer had told him that the number nine was his lucky number, and so he decided to replace several bank notes with denominations that are divisible by or include the number nine. Within hours people lost huge amounts of savings because their money became worthless. "We couldn't even afford one box of cigarettes," said democracy activist Ko Aung.

Popular anger grew and for most of 1988 Burma was shaken by some of the biggest protests the country had seen. The initial spark for the demonstrations was a brawl in the Sanda Win teashop, named after Ne Win's daughter, on 12th March, 1988, when students argued with the son of a senior government leader over what music to listen to. The brawl escalated and the following day, the police shot dead two of the students. This provoked street protests, which took in concerns not only over the shooting of the student but also over the demonetisation, and the shortages of essential goods and spiralling inflation.

Aung San Suu Kyi had for much her life been out of Burmese politics and society. She studied abroad and married Michael Aris, an Oxford academic. The family lived in Britain. However, in March 1988 her mother lay seriously ill in Rangoon, and Aung San Suu Kyi returned to her country to be by her mother's bedside. Little did the world know that she was walking into a political crisis that would change the course of her life.

The protests resulted in several brutal crackdowns. Ne Win went on air and said that "when soldiers shoot, they don't shoot into the air, they shoot straight". This was an echo of his warning in 1962 that "monks and students need to be hit hard". Tanks were sent in to crush the demonstrations. Students were drowned in the Inya Lake on 16th March. Forty-one people were suffocated to death in a prison van, driven around for two hours before being brought, dead, to Insein Prison. All the universities were closed down.[1]

In June, some campuses re-opened, but the students had not been cowed by the earlier crackdown, and they resumed their demonstrations. They demanded the release of other students and the right to establish student unions. On 20th June, Rangoon University was closed once again. On 21st June, 20,000 students, monks and workers demonstrated, and once again the Burma Army opened fire.

The protests were not exclusively Burman. Karens and other ethnic minorities who were living in the towns and cities participated too. Ner Soe, for example, was 19 and a student at the Technical Institute in Monywa. He spent time talking to individuals in the street, trying to establish some understanding of democracy. "We are prisoners in our own country, we are prisoners under the power of the military dictatorship," he said. "But before we can get democracy, we need to understand what it is and why we need it."

To the surprise of many, however, Ne Win then suddenly announced his resignation. Even more extraordinarily, he proposed holding a referendum on multi-party elections. He was replaced by the man who had overseen the crackdown on the demonstrations, Sein Lwin, known as the "Butcher of Rangoon", who declared martial law on 3rd August. Mass protests erupted in Rangoon, Mandalay, Moulmein and across Burma.

On 8th August, another day of demonstrations was held and this time the military reacted with the utmost brutality. It is estimated that on what is now known as "8-8-88" at least 3,000 people were shot dead. Four days later Sein Lwin resigned, and was replaced by the non-military, Western-educated Dr Maung Maung. Despite the massacre of demonstrators, protests continued, with 100,000 taking to the streets of Mandalay on 22nd August.[2] Dr Maung Maung's tenure was short, and he was replaced by General Saw Maung. The Orwellian-sounding State Law and Order Restoration Council (SLORC) was formed as the new government, and the slaughter of demonstrators continued. In the whole year, at least 10,000 people were killed. The United States, United Kingdom, Germany and Japan cut off all aid and Burma's destiny as a pariah state was sealed.

Thousands of protestors were rounded up and imprisoned, where they were subjected to extreme torture. Ko Aung, a Shan student and a founding member of the 150,000-strong All Burma Federation of Student Unions (ABFSU), was one of the first student leaders to be arrested. Military intelligence officials raided his home and took him away on 16th March. He was detained for a week in a cell with 140 others, beaten and tortured, and then released a month later. He was arrested again in September.

Ko Aung's ordeal began with a three-day interrogation, in which he was denied sleep. He was then held in military intelligence centres in Rangoon for six months, before being taken to the infamous Ye Kyi Aing prison. He was tied to a chair and beaten severely with a rubber rod. Policemen burned his chest with their cigarettes. The room was dark except for a light shining directly in his face. He was tied to the ceiling and spun round, a form of torture known as "the helicopter"; forced to crouch over an imaginary motorbike for hours, and denied sleep for a week. Interrogators rubbed a bamboo cane up and down his shins until the skin came off.

Worst of all, Ko Aung was led blindfolded with an iron chain around him down a path, and forced to climb into a ditch, about 20 feet deep and eight feet wide. In the ditch was a corpse, which in the sunshine began to decompose. At night the corpse turned cold. "I shivered and could not sleep, sitting next to the decomposing corpse," Ko Aung recalls. He stayed in the ditch for six days.

A week after this, Ko Aung was again taken from his cell at night, with a hood over his head and an iron chain on his wrist. He was put into a room with cages of wild birds – the bars of the cages were wide enough for the screaming birds, with their sharp beaks, to peck frenziedly at Ko Aung's body. "For one whole night I had to undergo this unbearable torture. My skin was shredded by the pecks of those birds, and covered in blood," he said.

As if this torture was not enough, Ko Aung received even worse treatment. Once again at night he was taken, blindfolded and chained, from his cell and led to a shed. His blindfold was taken off and he saw a circular pond, about six feet deep and eight feet wide. The pond was full of maggots from human waste. "I had to climb down the brick steps into the pool up to my neck," Ko Aung said. "When I got about three steps down, I began to feel and smell the liquid. Although I couldn't see anything, I knew it was the maggot pond. In the morning I saw the horrible maggots. They began crawling up to my face, mouth, nose, eyes and ears, making me cringe and shudder as my body itched with crawling maggots."

Ko Aung was tried on 9th April, 1990, with no defence lawyer available, and sentenced to seven years' hard labour in Insein Prison for "undermining the stability of the state". Here he endured yet more beatings and torture. He was held in solitary confinement for three years, kept in leg irons three times and beaten with pipes, sticks and bamboo canes. In 1994 he was finally released.

Aung Din was a student at the Rangoon Institute of Technology, who also became involved in organising the demonstrations. He too was arrested and sentenced to four years' imprisonment. "When I forgot to stand to attention, I was forced to crawl on sharp, pointed stones for 100 yards while the prison guards beat me with sticks and belts," he recalls. "Many of my fellow prisoners were tortured even more. They were tortured for dropping a cup of water. They were tortured for teaching English. They were tortured for anything. Often, when I tried to sleep, I could hear the screams of those being tortured. If there is a hell on earth, it must be Burma's Insein Prison where I was jailed."[3]

Despite the carnage of 1988, there were two positive outcomes of the events of that year. The first was the new-found role for Aung San Suu Kyi; the second was the new-found unity among the democracy groups and the ethnic armed resistance.

Aung San Suu Kyi always knew that, as her father's daughter, she may be called upon to play a role in the affairs of her home country. Whether she believed she would get involved so quickly in the democracy struggle when she went home to nurse her mother, and whether she knew she might not get out again, is uncertain, although Ko Aung believes she had already made her decision. "She was ready for it. She was ready to take up a leadership role, but only if the people asked her to. She needed the people's mandate," said Ko Aung. That mandate came quickly and within a few months of returning to Rangoon, she took a leading role in the uprising. On 26th August, she addressed a crowd of 500,000 people on the slopes of Shwedagon Hill[4] and her political struggle began.

Since 1988, Aung San Suu Kyi has been in and out of house arrest. She was released from a period of house arrest in 2002, and in September that year she made the following statement:

> My release does not mean release for all the people in Burma . . . The people are desperate for change. They all know that there should be a better world waiting for them and in my opinion, our people deserve a better world because they have the right sort of spirit. They have hope and they know what they want. The only thing they do not know is how they could get what they want. In order to get what they want, they need help . . . What they want is not wrong, what they want is security, justice. They want progress, they want prosperity. They want all the basic things that ordinary human beings want. They are not asking for too much, they are just asking for very simple things.

After the massacres and arrests, at least 10,000 Burman democracy activists, mostly students, fled to the Thai–Burmese border, and another 2,000 escaped to Kachin areas in northern Burma. At least 6,000 people sought refuge with the Karen and Mon resistance forces. Their journey to the border was long and arduous.

Ner Soe, a Karen himself, fled to the border. He started off by car, a four hour drive to Pin Sa Loke. From there he walked for one week through the jungle and across mountains, to Manerplaw, where he joined the KNLA. It is the armed struggle that gives him hope. "We Karen are still trying, still sacrificing in the front line," he said. "The Karen soldiers are stronger than me, they sacrifice more than me. Even when they are very poor, and have not enough equipment or food, they are still fighting. The ones in the front line – they are my hope." Ner Soe also finds inspiration from Scripture, he told me. "The biggest hope for me is the promise of God. Psalm 2 verse 8 – 'Ask of me and I will make the nations your inheritance, the ends of the earth your possession' – gives me hope."

The uprising in 1988 was by no means the first, but it was the first to draw international attention. The student movement in Burma started in 1920 with demonstrations against the British occupation. Under Ne Win's rule, protests were organised in 1962, 1973, 1974, 1975, 1976, 1978 and 1987. Aung Saw Oo had been a participant in most of these demonstrations, and had been imprisoned twice. During the early 1980s he served thirteen months in solitary confinement, and went on hunger strike. On his first hunger strike, he had no food or water for six days. His second hunger strike lasted ten days. "My stomach and kidneys were damaged as a result," he said.

Maung Kyaw was also involved in several of the pre-1988 protests. A Burman, he is now married to a Karen and works for the Karen cause, representing them in Germany. "I was born in the jungle, in the middle of a battle," said Maung Kyaw. "Because of the nature of the battle, exactly where I was born I am not sure." In 1969 Maung Kyaw, a marine biology student in Moulmein, became involved in the University Golden Jubilee movement's protests against the Ne Win regime, in which the demonstrators occupied a university compound for three days. The university was closed down and all the students were sent home. Then, they were arrested.

"I was arrested at midnight," Maung Kyaw recalls. "They came and surrounded my house, and took me to the police station. I saw two of my friends, but they separated us. They blindfolded me and kept me in solitary confinement for two months. I did not know day or night. I only realised it was two months when I was released." He was subjected to mental torture – put in a room full of bugs and forbidden to kill the bugs – and sometimes denied sleep. Finally, he was released, after being forced to sign a statement promising not to be involved with any political activities at all in the future. He was also expelled from university.

A year later, however, Maung Kyaw was, surprisingly, offered the opportunity to appeal to resume his studies, and his application was granted. He was not allowed to live on campus, and was still viewed with suspicion by the authorities, but at the same time, his old friends lost their trust in him – they believed he had compromised himself and perhaps even become an informer. "I was a total outsider."

He completed his education and found a job in the Forestry Department. Then came 1988. "By this time, I had a family and two sons. I was quite settled in my life, I was the owner of a saw mill, and I hesitated about becoming involved again. I tried to stay out of it," he explained. "But because the government was stupid and corrupt, I could not avoid getting involved. Most demonstrators were students and nobody could control them except for me. It was not because of politics that I got involved, it was because of friendship." Maung Kyaw became the leader in Toungoo, and played a key role in preventing violent acts of revenge by the students. "After the military crackdown on 19th September, 1988, I was wanted by the military intelligence. So I went into hiding."

Maung Kyaw fled to the Thai–Burmese border and joined the KNLA. He served as a soldier in the jungle for two years and then, when his base was overrun by the Burma Army in 1990, he crossed into Thailand. "I hid in the jungle on the Thai side without any food or medicine for almost a month. My wife's situation worsened – she was not prepared for such a life. We lost everything."

He decided to get his wife to safety, and so he bought a fake passport in Thailand and flew to Germany. "But I hadn't seen a passport in my life before, and I didn't know what a visa meant," he said. "With all these fake documents, I was arrested in Frankfurt airport."

At this point, a Christian missionary group in Frankfurt stepped in. "We were about to be sent back, but one young

Thousands of Karen are displaced, on the run, fleeing through the jungle from the Burma Army. (Photo: Free Burma Rangers)

Carrying their worldly possessions with them, Karen people move from one location across a river to another to escape attack. (Photo: Free Burma Rangers)

With little to eat, no shelter and no medicines, trapped in the jungle with children to look after, these Karen women rest for a few moments. (Photo: Free Burma Rangers)

A Free Burma Ranger medic, known as "The Mad Dog", examining a Karen internally displaced child in the jungle. (Photo: Free Burma Rangers)

The internally displaced people in the jungles often die of treatable disease because of lack of medical care. The Free Burma Rangers deliver medicines and treatment. (Photo: Free Burma Rangers)

The Dooplaya Massacre 2002. Twelve villagers were murdered in Htee Law Bleh on April 28th, 2002. Over 5,000 Karen were displaced in Dooplaya district between April and June 2002, six villages burned, five churches destroyed and three pastors captured and tortured. (Photo: Free Burma Rangers)

A typical Karen village. (Photo: Free Burma Rangers)

A village on the banks of the Moei river after an attack by the Burma Army. (Photo: Christopher Chan)

In a Karen village in the jungle, this banner poses a challenge to us all. (Photo: Benedict Rogers)

Despite the suffering, Karen Christians exude a joy and faithfulness in their worship that is humbling. (Photo: Free Burma Rangers)

A Global Day of Prayer for Burma takes place on the second Sunday of every March, organised by Christians Concerned for Burma. The Karen Christians themselves participate, in their jungle hide-outs and villages. (Photo: Free Burma Rangers)

The Free Burma Rangers teach a jungle Sunday school. (Photo: Free Burma Rangers)

Prayer and Baptism: Karen soldiers accept the Lord and are baptised in the river. (Photo: Christopher Chan)

Joyful children: Karen children are like children anywhere – able to smile and play and laugh, despite the adversity. (Photo: Free Burma Rangers)

ABSDF & KNLA, "Comrades in Arms". A major breakthrough for the opposition groups came when the pro-democracy students fled to the Karen areas near the Thai border, formed the All Burma Students Democratic Front (ABSDF), and trained and fought alongside Karen National Liberation Army (KNLA) soldiers. These soldiers are in Bo Bo Taw Village in the KNLA's 6th Brigade area, in 1996. (Photo: Hamilton Walters)

Pastor Jerry Lin: "The foreigners that have helped us are the modern-day Moses and Esthers," said Pastor Jerry Lin. (Photo: Hamilton Walters, Mae La refugee camp, 2003)

Saw Ba U Gyi, the "father" of the Karen revolution, was a British-trained barrister who spoke fluent English and studied Latin. A committed Christian, "he believed in doing unto others as you would others do unto you," said his daughter, Thelma Gyi-Baerlein. (Source: Thelma Gyi-Baerlein)

General Bo Mya – the leader of the Karen armed resistance for almost 40 years. A Seventh Day Adventist and a staunch anti-communist. (Photo: Benedict Rogers)

man arranged everything for us. We were held in the police station for a week trying to explain the situation to the German police. The policeman told me that the only way we could avoid being deported at once was to apply for political asylum. I asked what 'political asylum' meant. Three years later, I was recognised as a political refugee."

An initial stumbling block, however, was that the police could not understand how Maung Kyaw and his wife had left Burma without valid travel documents. "They asked how we came to Thailand, and we said by foot. 'Is that possible?' they asked. We told them that we had walked through the jungle for ten days and then crossed the border. 'How did you cross the border?' they asked. 'By boat,' we told them. 'Is that possible without any documents?' they asked. 'Yes, it is possible,' we said."

Maung Kyaw's asylum hearing was held, paradoxically, in Nuremburg. "When I was in Burma I used to say that the regime should be brought to trial in Nuremburg, but in fact I was the one who ended up on trial in Nuremburg," said Maung Kyaw.

For the Burman democracy activists and the Karen 1988 was a turning point, a "unifying moment". Maung Kyaw is now deeply committed to the Karen cause, and feels disappointed with those Burman democracy activists who returned to Rangoon from the border after a few years and betrayed their Karen hosts. "They forgot how they lived, the reason they are still alive. For me, the Karen gave me shelter, food and that is why I survived. Now I have a good life, and I have to give something back," he said. Furthermore, his wife is Karen. "I am a Burman. They say that Karens are second-class citizens. But what about my wife and sons? I have to do something for the image of my sons and my wife."

Since his escape to Germany, Maung Kyaw has returned to the Karen areas fourteen times, making trips deep inside the jungle to deliver medicines and gather information. On one visit, he met an elderly Karen lady, displaced in the jungle bereft of food, who asked what he was doing for the cause in Germany. He told her they had held a demonstration at the Burmese Embassy. "Does it work?" she asked. "We'll do more," he said. "Maybe we will have a hunger strike." She looked shocked. "My son, that doesn't work," she said. "We have been doing that for years and it doesn't work."

Although by his upbringing he is a Buddhist, Maung Kyaw's wife is a Christian and he believes in God. "I strongly believe in the will of God. I believe the words of God are the way of life. I don't know what God looks like, but I believe in Jesus Christ."

On 5th November, 1988 the All Burma Students Democratic Front (ABSDF) was formed at the KNU base in Kawmoorah, and the students took up arms and joined the KNU forces in the trenches. This was perhaps the best example of collaboration between the Karen and the Burman democracy forces. Several times in the past alliances had been built between the different ethnic nationalities, but seldom had the ethnic groups joined forces with the Burman resistance groups. An agreement between the Karen and the Burmese Communist Party was reached in 1952, but anticommunist feelings among the Karen made that alliance a tense one. 1988 brought people together as never before.

Initially the Karen, and their ethnic resistance allies in the National Democratic Front (NDF), had mixed feelings about the presence of the students in their territory. While the KNU and NDF were willing to house and look after the students, and to provide military training for those who wanted to take up arms, some among them were sceptical. This was partly due to age-old racial hostilities between the Karens and the Burmans, but it was also based on the valid opinion that one "can't become a guerrilla overnight".[5]

Min Zaw Oo, one of the students who fled to the border, said that relations were strained at first. "It was a bumpy ride," he claimed. "The Karens did not trust the Burmans and were suspicious of 'communists'. Sometimes the Karens executed students they believed to be leftists. But eventually the problems were sorted out and it paved the way for co-operation. The students were put right in the front line of fighting, and they built trust among the Karen by being willing to fight. The alliance between the ethnic nationalities and the Burman democracy activists was unprecedented historically."

Moe Thee Zun, who along with his childhood friend Min Ko Naing led the student movement and became chairman of the ABSDF a year after its establishment, told the Karens in the jungle that the students were simply "another ethnic group" in Burma. He recalled that tensions emerged as a result of simpler issues than politics, and were easily resolved. "You can study a lot about human nature when you're in the jungle, or in prison. For example, when the ABSDF students who were living with Karen soldiers brushed their teeth in the morning, the Karen soldiers got annoyed because they did not have tooth brushes, and felt the students were acting superior," he said. "The solution was to provide tooth brushes for everyone. Once we did that, we all became good friends. It was easier than federalism!" Moe Thee Zun, who founded the Democratic Party for a New Society to contest the 1990 elections, and re-organised the student unions into the All Burma Federation of Student Unions (ABFSU), said that as a result of his time living in the jungle with the Karen, he developed a deep commitment to federalism. "The solution for the ethnic problem is to establish a truly federal system. That is not just my political outlook, it comes from my heart after living with the ethnic groups."

Aung Saw Oo, who took part in joint operations on Sleeping Dog Mountain, remembers some tensions at lower

levels, but the KNU and NDF leadership were very generous
to the students. "They were very welcoming. It was the first
time for non-Burmans and Burmans to join each other in a
struggle, and it gave us the opportunity to understand each
other," he said. "We understood each other in the battlefield.
But at lower levels, there was some narrow-minded chauvin-
ism because of past experiences. They hated the Burmans. We
explained to them that when the Burma Army destroys their
villages, it is not Burmans, it is the regime."

Nevertheless, an alliance emerged and ABSDF soldiers took
part in joint operations with KNLA troops. Perhaps for the
first time, some of the Burman democracy activists saw the
reality of the suffering that the Karen had endured for so many
years. "The Karen and Karenni have sacrificed more than any
other group in Burma," Kho Than Khe, the ABSDF Chairman, told me in 2003. "They are fighting for their dignity."

Two years after the uprising in Burma, the regime decided
to hold elections. It is unclear why they reached this decision,
but perhaps they believed that by appearing to introduce
democracy, they could quell public discontent, and at the same
time through intimidation they could secure a mandate
through the ballot box which would legitimise their rule. They
also thought that the opposition vote would be split among
the hundreds of parties which registered. Whatever their
thinking, they badly miscalculated.

Even though Aung San Suu Kyi was placed under house
arrest and banned from running in the election, and despite
the arrest of over 6,000 political activists across the country
and the release of 7,000 common criminals to make room for
them in the jails,[6] the junta was roundly defeated. It had tried
to distort the outcome from the beginning, by banning party
emblems, restricting television and radio appearances for
opposition candidates, and maintaining martial law.[7] According to Aung Saw Oo, the parties were not allowed to hold

gatherings of more than 50 people, were forbidden to use loudspeakers and were banned from publishing literature. Furthermore, the democracy movement appeared badly disorganised and divided, with the registration of 234 different parties, but ultimately the people spoke through the ballot box. "The conditions were not free and fair," said Aung Saw Oo. "Only on the final day, when counting the vote, was it free and fair." The National League for Democracy (NLD), led by Aung San Suu Kyi, won over 80 per cent of the parliamentary seats.

Despite General Saw Maung's promise on 9th January, 1990 that the military would respect the election results and hand over power to an elected government, the regime reneged on its promise. Finding the results not to its liking, the SLORC – soon to be renamed State Peace and Development Council (SPDC) on the advice of public relations consultants – disregarded the outcome and imprisoned the victors of the election.

The years since 1990 have been little but years of deadlock and oppression. Min Ko Naing, one of the main student leaders, remains in solitary confinement in prison, having been arrested in 1989. Occasionally the door creaks open and a little light gets in. Occasionally some political prisoners, of whom there are over 1,500 still behind bars, are released and there is talk of "dialogue" between the regime and the NLD. But before any progress is made, the door slams shut again and the democrats are jailed once more.

In May 2002, Aung San Suu Kyi was released from house arrest. But a year later, after she had travelled around the country attracting huge crowds, the junta became nervous. In the most ruthless crackdown since 1988, they sent in thugs to attack her convoy on 30th May, 2003 and arrested hundreds of her followers. Agents dressed as monks, and armed soldiers and police attacked the convoy with guns, bamboo stakes,

catapults and steel pipes. Hundreds went missing and many
were killed. Daw Suu Kyi herself was arrested again, and was
taken to an undisclosed location for several months, before
being moved back to her house and held there under house
arrest.

Meanwhile, the democracy movement and the ethnic
groups continue their struggle. In the aftermath of the elections, some elected Members of Parliament were arrested,
while others went into hiding. Some escaped to the border
areas and into exile.

Lian Uk, a Chin Christian, was elected MP for Hakha, Chin
State, and then had to go into months of hiding. He was in
trouble not only as a democratic politician, but also because
he had drafted a constitution for Chin State, calling for a
federal Burma. In January 1991 his photograph was published
in the newspapers with a notice for his arrest. "People in the
neighbourhood in which I was hiding came up to me with the
newspaper and said 'This is you, isn't it?'" he recalls. "'No
no,' I told them. 'It's just someone who looks a bit like me!'
But I knew I couldn't stay there. I moved from place to place."
He had already been in prison from 1972 until 1974, for proposing a federal system. The prison conditions were terrible.
"Having been in jail once, I completely tried to avoid any possibility of going to jail again," he said.

Miraculously, at every checkpoint between Rangoon and the
Indian border, the soldiers were either absent or distracted, and
Lian Uk escaped. He had some close encounters. In one village
he was hiding in the house of a woman he did not know at all
– and she was not at home. Suddenly he heard that the police
were coming, so he hid in her bedroom. At that point she came
home, found a stranger in her bedroom, and screamed. But
remarkably, Lian Uk's friends managed to distract the police,
chatting to them and telling jokes, and the police dismissed the
woman's complaints and went on their way.

On 18th December, 1990, Aung San Suu Kyi's cousin, former university mathematics lecturer Dr Sein Win and some other democratic politicians who had escaped arrest, fled to Manerplaw and formed the National Coalition Government of the Union of Burma (NCGUB), a government in exile. In 1992, the NDF, DAB, NCGUB and the NLD "Liberated Areas" met in Manerplaw and agreed a common platform of a federal union of Burma, and formed the National Council of the Union of Burma (NCUB).[8] And in 1997, the ethnic nationalities came together and signed the Mae Tha Raw Hta Agreement, in which they pledged to "dismantle the military dictatorship" and "join hands with the pro-democracy forces led by Aung San Suu Kyi".[9]

The events of 1988 also caused the defection of a dozen Burmese diplomats around the world. In February 1989, U Maung Kyi, the Third Secretary in the Burmese Embassy in London, defected. He had already started to raise questions with his superiors about the way events were being handled in Rangoon, and this had alerted the authorities to a potential problem. "I was suspicious when I was recalled home before anybody was organised to replace me," he said. "If I went I would be tortured. They would take out my eyes, then my teeth. Then they would kill me."[10] An Arakanese, U Maung Kyi now works for the democracy movement and the Arakan ethnic nationality's struggle from London.

Although the picture seems bleak, the events of 1988 and 1990 had the positive effect of drawing more attention to the suffering of the people of Burma, and attracting to the cause high calibre Burmese who had gone abroad in the early days of Ne Win. Men like Harn Yawnghwe.

Born into one of the oldest aristocratic Shan Buddhist families, and the son of the first President of Burma who was imprisoned by Ne Win, Harn Yawnghwe spent much of his childhood and education in Thailand and Canada. It was there that he became a Christian, in 1976. "I wanted to find a faith," he explains. "I tried to live as a Buddhist, because all Shans are Buddhists. But the more I learned about Buddhism, the more I felt that if I really wanted to live as a true Buddhist, I would need to be a hermit and be away from the distractions of the world. I didn't think I could do that, so I thought the next best thing was to be a capitalist, a millionaire. So I went to business school, and got a job in investment. But I got bored with money."

Harn Yawnghwe searched for meaning in life, but was sceptical about Christianity. "I was very much a self-made man. I felt I could do anything, I didn't need God, a family, or anybody else," he said. "But then a strange thing happened. I was approaching the end of my Masters of Business Administration (MBA) and if you have an engineering degree and an MBA, that was your ticket – everybody wanted you. But, while all my friends were getting job offers, including some classmates who couldn't speak English properly, I couldn't get a job. I was a Canadian citizen, but an Australian friend got a job in Canada before me. For six months I looked around for a job, and began to question my own ability."

Another blow to Harn Yawnghwe's self-esteem came when he met a woman whom he found attractive. He asked her for a date, and was shocked when she said no. She was a Christian, had grown up in a missionary family in Malaysia, and she told him that the Bible says believers should not be yoked with unbelievers. "I couldn't believe that she could live according to this book! I was very upset."

In his anger, he decided to investigate this Christianity that was stopping this girl dating him. He went to a Chinese church, and the pastor preached systematically on the Gospel of Matthew. "It was fascinating. I started reading the New Testament. Finally I concluded that there must be a God. But I was still not convinced about Jesus."

However, something from his Shan heritage came back to haunt him. In Burma, there is a widespread and powerful belief in spiritual beings known as "nats". There is a mountain in Burma, Mount Popa, which is the home of the nats, and the jungle, land and water are believed to be full of nats. "I thought that if this Jesus was not really God, but I accepted him as God, one of these nats would come and get me!" he explained.

There then followed an extraordinary spiritual experience. One day he was sitting in his apartment, and he saw a vision of a little child entering the room. "When I tried to touch it, something inside told me it was evil. I saw something push me right down on the couch. I didn't know what to do, but the pastor had been preaching about Legion, the spirits and the swine, so in my fear I said 'In the name of Jesus go away'. It went. So I thought maybe Jesus really does have the power."

Ultimately, Harn Yawnghwe tried to strike a deal with God. "I told him that if He would give me a job, I would believe in Him. But I still didn't get a job, so I started to talk with my friends about it," he said. "They said to me that if God was really real, would I dare to talk to Him like that? Would I talk to the Prime Minister like that? I agreed, and so that night I prayed for the first time. I said I just want to know whether there is a God or not. I said I didn't care whether I ever saw the woman I wanted to date again, I didn't care if I would have to go back to Burma, I just wanted to know if He really is God, and if He is, I would serve Him. The next morning the telephone rang with a job interview, a week later I was called for a second interview, and that same day they offered me the job. There had been at least 50 applicants." The woman he had wanted to date is now his wife.

A little while after becoming a Christian, Harn left the business world and worked for World Vision in Thailand, and with the Bible Society in Hong Kong. Then, in 1987, he read an economic report about the crisis in Burma. "I got very angry because after 25 years of military rule, they had messed up the economy. I wondered what I should do," he said. He left the Bible Society in 1988, and began to get involved in the Burmese democracy movement from overseas. He advised the Canadian Government on developments in Burma, and then in 1990 founded the Euro-Burma Office in Brussels.

His conversion drew initial controversy among the Buddhist Shan and Burman communities. "My brother said that my family would disown me. I said 'OK, why not?' He asked how I could take it so lightly, and I said I was not taking it lightly, but that if they did disown me I would accept it, because I believed in God." His family did not disown him, although many Shans believed he had betrayed his people by becoming a Christian. He was also viewed with suspicion by Shans for working with the Burman democracy groups. However, these suspicions have started to be overcome. "Whether someone is Buddhist, Christian, Burman, Shan, whatever, I will always work with them for the cause of democracy in Burma. And while I never talk about my faith unless people ask me, I hope that through my actions something of my faith in Christ comes through."

The Christian faith of others who campaign for freedom and democracy in Burma shines through too. Dr Salai Tun Than is one example. A 74-year-old retired Chin university professor, he was arrested in November 2001 for handing out a letter urging the regime to stop perpetrating injustice, and to introduce basic civil liberties, democracy, and respect for human dignity to Burma. In his letter, he wrote this:

Many potential intellectuals of our high schools and universities have already been killed. It is about time that you kill an old professor . . . It is about time to stop killing your kinsfolk. If you join us you all will be adored by the people. Let us rewrite our tarnished history together . . . If you consider that you cannot agree with me, please don't hesitate. Go ahead and kill me. I will be here all the time. I will forgive my killers from the bottom of my heart.

He continued in the same vein:

If we happen to meet together . . . and if I were a mighty person and you all were weaklings and if I find you naked, starved, stricken with sores and diseases and lost in the darkness of your existence in tears, may I kindly wipe away your tears and feed you, clothe you, and make you whole from your diseases and sores and give you hope with reality of well-being in your lives. May God bless and forgive my killers.

Aung San Suu Kyi has acquired legendary status – she is now an icon of the struggle. Her cousin Dr Sein Win, Prime Minister of the NCGUB in exile in the United States, believes this is partly because she is Aung San's daughter, but it is also because of her own personal example. "People have total trust in her as a leader who will stand with the people," he said. Aung Saw Oo, whom she appointed as a divisional organiser for the NLD, believes it is because she is "very open-minded and very disciplined" that she has won such unanimous support from people. But some, wisely, urge caution in placing all hope on one individual. "We should not hope that someone can be totally responsible for the improvement of our life," said Maung Kyaw. "We must try by ourselves."

Mahn Ba Zan said that one of the problems has been that "the Karen revolutionary and Burmese revolutionary or rebellious forces had no understanding, nor liaison, between one another". For this reason there were "no united efforts but rather separate and individual endeavours". He continued: "I am convinced that the combined efforts of these forces could have completely defeated the common enemy . . . A very good opportunity for the revolution has been lost."[11]

Perhaps, finally, Mahn Ba Zan's vision is beginning to be shared by other ethnic leaders and Burmese democracy activists. Efforts are being made to increase co-operation, for they all, ultimately, share the same goal. The Christian Kachin, who rose up in 1960 in protest at U Nu's decision to make Buddhism the state religion, desire autonomy just as much as the Buddhist Shan. The Karenni, who were never part of Burma before the Burmans invaded in 1948, have perhaps the best claim to independence, having been granted sovereign rights in perpetuity in a treaty with the British in 1875, but they do not rule out federalism. The Chin, Mon, Arakan and Karen all seek a federal, democratic Burma. Several draft constitutions have been written by different groups, but they all contain similar provisions for a federal Burma in which the rights of all ethnic nationalities are protected. In contrast, the SPDC has drafted a constitution in which the Burma Army retains the right to a quarter of the seats in a future parliament, and the power to appoint a President and Vice-President from the military. Clearly such a constitution is unacceptable to all democratic forces. The army must be taken out of politics, and placed under the control of an elected, civilian government. All the forces of opposition to the evil regime in Rangoon can unite around that goal, to bring an end to tyranny and build a new, free and just Burma.

NOTES

1 Martin Smith, *Burma: Insurgency and the Politics of Ethnicity*, p. 2
2 Ibid., p. 5
3 Aung Din, Testimony to the Congressional Human Rights Caucus, Washington DC, June 19th, 2003
4 Smith, p. 8
5 Ibid., p. 17

6 Ibid., p. 23
7 Ibid., p. 412
8 Ibid., p. 444
9 Ibid., p. 431
10 *Daily Mail*, February 13th, 1989
11 Mahn Ba Zan, biography by Robert Zan, p. 92

CHAPTER FIVE

THE MONK AND THE GENERALS

"Be completely humble and gentle;
be patient, bearing with one another in love.
Make every effort to keep the unity of the Spirit
through the bond of peace."
Ephesians 4:2–3

Twelve-year-old Hope sat among the huge crowd gathered in the parade ground in Manerplaw, and listened to the leaders' announcements. The Burma Army had already started to shell the areas nearby, and was closing in. People were starting to gather what possessions they could carry in preparation for an escape. Hope's mother told her she had to pack one spare set of clothes, and fill a long hosepipe-like container with rice to take with them.

That night, all the inhabitants of Manerplaw fled. They slept in the jungle on the ground, with no mat or mosquito net. "It was a full moon," Hope recalls. "No one could sleep. We were worried about snakes, and about the Burmans." In the distance, Manerplaw was ablaze, destroyed not by the Burma Army, but by the Karen who did not want to leave any materials or resources behind which might aid their enemy.

Manerplaw was the Karen headquarters from 1975 until it fell in 1995. But it was not just the Karen base. For several years it was also the centre of activities for the National Democratic Front (NDF), the Democratic Alliance of Burma (DAB), the All Burma Students Democratic Front (ABSDF), the National Coalition Government of the Union of Burma (NCGUB) and various other ethnic and Burman alliances in the struggle for democracy. It became known as the "last stronghold of democracy in Burma".

Its fall in 1995 was a major blow to the resistance. Not only was it the command centre of operations for 20 years, but it was also the last remaining symbol of strength for an increasingly beleaguered resistance. And it need not have happened. The Karen lost Manerplaw because they allowed an internal split to develop, and they gave the SPDC the opportunity to exploit that split. Indeed, the SPDC sought to make the divisions wider and deeper, and turn the Karen factions against each other. Ultimately, they succeeded in this goal. As Colonel Nerdah Mya said, "Once the SPDC see a crack in the opposition, they make it bigger."

The Karen leadership is predominantly Christian, but the majority of Karen people, and the front line soldiers in the KNLA, are still Buddhist. Traditionally the Buddhists and Christians had little strife, and worked together for the Karen cause. But in the late 1980s, frustration grew among the Buddhist Karen – and among rank-and-file Christians too – that the Karen Christian leaders were living a relatively comfortable existence by the river in Manerplaw, while the Buddhist soldiers fought the war. According to Christian Goodden, some Buddhist soldiers believed they were being passed over for promotion because they were not Christians.[1]

Some Karen leaders admitted that this was true. After the fall of Manerplaw, the Health Minister, Dr Po Thaw Da, told his friend Dr Martin Panter, an English doctor who had been working among the Karen since 1989, that the Karen needed more prayer. "Some of our leaders look to themselves and care more for themselves than they do for their people," he said. "Please pray that they will repent and be prepared to work together in true love and humility, and maybe God will restore us. Pray also for reconciliation between Buddhists and Christians. There is hostility because of what has happened, and only humility and love will restore these broken relationships."[2]

Dr Panter found that in the previous ten years 80 per cent of the new recruits to the KNLA had been Buddhists, and two-thirds of those on the front line were Buddhist. The ratio in the leadership in Manerplaw was, however, reversed with two-thirds of the senior officers being Christian.

Furthermore there had been, according to Dr Panter, some mismanagement of funds by the Karen leadership. Some leaders admitted that, for example, a ceremony which cost 5,000 Baht was recorded in the accounts as 6,000 Baht. The transfer of a patient to a Thai hospital cost 2,000 Baht but was recorded as 3,000 Baht. "It was generally in small amounts, but in a dishonest fashion," Dr Panter wrote in his report.[3] In both cases the difference had been pocketed by an official.

Conditions for the Buddhist troops on the front line, of course, were tough. They remained at their posts for two or three months at a time without any relief, and their food rations of rice and chilli were minimal. "Rumours had been circulating for some months (some of them in fact true) that special provisions that had been given by concerned donors from overseas, for instance chocolates, candies and cigarettes, which had been specifically designated for front line troops were not getting through to them, but were being creamed off or simply appropriated by officials at Manerplaw," noted Dr Panter.[4]

Min Zaw Oo, a Burman student who had fled to the border in 1988 and worked with the Karens, confirms this. "There was no big animosity between Christians and Buddhists in the villages. The source of the problem was the distribution of wealth and power among the Karen," he said. "The remedy would have been to distribute resources wisely and proportionately. Through teak deals, many of the senior Karen Christian officers grew rich, while the front line troops remained poor." Another problem, Min Zaw Oo felt, was that the Karen have not been good at promoting young, forward-looking leaders. "The 'younger' generation of leadership is between 55 and 60."

All of this, left unchecked as it was, gave the junta the opportunity to strike. The SPDC had its sights set on Manerplaw for some time. In 1989 it had launched a major offensive, crossing into Thai territory and attacking the Karen from the rear, and had captured camps at Klerday, Maw Po, Phalu and Three Pagodas Pass. In early 1992 the junta launched "Operation Dragon King", a full scorched-earth policy in all Karen areas, targeting Manerplaw and Kawmoora. On 6th January, 1992, General Bo Mya had called for a day of prayer and fasting. Dr Panter's wife Sally recorded in her diary that: "We have arrived here to find much fighting around. Morale is high among the Karen but they are also very tired. There was a major attack planned for Manerplaw on Sunday but we believe that because of the prayer and fasting it was held back. The Karen are digging trenches in Htoo Wah Lu as the Thais have said that the Burmese can bomb two miles into Thailand – thus much of the Karen territory."

On 18th March, 1992, the KNU Foreign Office issued a plea for help. "We appeal to the international community to defend Manerplaw . . . Burma's capital for freedom," the KNU statement read. It went unanswered, but the KNU saw off the threat at that time by itself.

However, having failed to conquer Manerplaw militarily, either by land or through aerial bombardment, the SPDC changed tack. In late 1994 they sent in agents to start spreading rumours about corruption among the Christian Karen leadership, and they also sent Buddhist missionaries to monasteries in the area. A monk, Myiang Gyi Ngu Sayadaw, or U Thu Zana, started to stir up trouble, and it is widely believed that he was being backed by the SPDC. He had moved into the area in 1992 from Ka Ka Maung township, 20 kilometres away. In 1992, Sally Panter noted that the SPDC was already "trying to win over the Buddhist priest, calling the people to turn back to Buddha". They also imprisoned, tortured and killed many Karen Christian pastors.

The monk started to build a monastery at Thu-Mwe-Hta, which became known as the River Junction Pagoda,[5] on the confluence of the Moie and Salween rivers, and called all Buddhist Karens, including soldiers, to help with the construction. He also started to build other monasteries in other parts of Kawthoolei. This, of course, depleted the KNLA forces.

After the monastery was completed, the monk then taught the Buddhist soldiers that they should not serve in the KNLA, and that they should not kill the Burmans – they should be neutral. Even those soldiers who disregarded that teaching were summoned for prayer at the monastery at times which were not convenient to the armed struggle. On one occasion, a night when there was a full moon and the Buddhists were required to pray, a KNLA commander ordered his men to stay where they were and not go back to the monastery. Two soldiers, however, disobeyed orders and sneaked out. When their superiors found them, they punished them with a beating.

This only served to exacerbate the division. The news got out, and the monk started to claim that the KNLA leaders were oppressing the Buddhists. In Colonel Nerdah Mya's view, this was absolutely untrue but "some people were not well-educated and were misled by this information. The misinformation spread rapidly".

The monk's cult status grew and rumours spread that he had supernatural powers, that he could fly, raise all the money that was needed and feed everybody. More Buddhist Karen went to the monastery to hear the monk's teachings. Initially, 40 KNLA soldiers defected, joining the monk's movement. It grew to 600.

Despite preaching non-violence, the monk turned his movement into an armed force. On 1st December, 1994 the monk, along with a soldier named Khaw Then and about 30 of their followers blocked the river and halted all traffic. The KNU earned its meagre revenues from a four per cent tax on border trade coming through its territory, and from the teak trade, so the monk's act was damaging the KNU's livelihood. Boats that refused to stop were fired on. Accusing the Christians of systematic oppression of Buddhists, he arrested five Christian Karen soldiers and tortured them severely. They were given a choice of converting to Buddhism or dying. When they held firm to their Christian faith, they were executed. Taking eight boats, he led his men to Manerplaw and attempted to disarm the KNLA. They were stopped, but fierce fighting broke out.

The Karen leadership decided to negotiate with the monk and his men, and on 7th December a team of 16 officials, including seven Buddhist soldiers who had stayed loyal to the KNLA, went to meet them. A Thai Buddhist monk agreed to act as an independent observer. The negotiators promised no recriminations and sought simply to reach a peaceful agreement. They also agreed to address the Buddhists' grievances. However, seven of the negotiators, including a Buddhist monk from Manerplaw and Mahn Sha, a Buddhist, were taken hostage by U Thu Zana.[6]

Eight days later the hostages were released and the Buddhist faction agreed to work out an agreement. Traffic resumed on the river. However, on 28th December the faction started to loot and steal from Thai and Karen boats on the river, and they issued a statement announcing their collective resignations from the KNU and accusing the KNU of religious oppression. The monk tried to portray the conflict as a Buddhist–Christian conflict, and appealed to all Karen Buddhists to join the struggle against the Christians. A fully fledged army was born, the Democratic Karen Buddhist Army (DKBA), which then joined forces with the SPDC. A political wing, the Democratic Karen Buddhist Organisation (DKBO) was also established. On 3rd January, 1995 the KNLA declared war on the DKBA/DKBO, but its grip on Manerplaw was already starting to unravel.

From its very beginning, the DKBA was an instrument in the Burmese junta's hands. Pastor Simon, a Karen theologian, said he wanted to tell the DKBA that their name was misleading. "They say they are democratic, but do they know about democracy? They say they are Karen, but why do they kill Karen people? They say they are Buddhist, but the four noble truths of Buddhism teach people to do good. And they say they are an army, but an army should only fight with an enemy, not with civilians," he said. "But maybe they were drunk and would not listen. So instead I prayed that God would put fear in their hearts."

The SPDC moved many more battalions into the area, and the DKBA provided the SPDC with invaluable intelligence. On 20th January, SPDC and DKBA forces captured White Mountain, which overlooked Manerplaw. They knew what areas were mined and which were not, which paths to take to get to Manerplaw safely. They led the SPDC to Manerplaw, and the KNLA retreated on 26th January. Six other bases, to the north and south of Manerplaw, also fell. "It was a mess," recalls Colonel Nerdah Mya. "People were running for their lives. Many more refugees fled across the border. More refugee camps had to be set up." The KNLA force of 15,000 was reduced to about a third of its size, through defections and widespread resignations by disillusioned soldiers.

Colonel Nerdah Mya acknowledges that the KNLA leadership made some mistakes. "They could have done more to emphasise that it was not a Buddhist–Christian war, that it was to do with politics," he said. "They could have done more to emphasise that we have to work together in unity."

Less than a month after the fall of Manerplaw, the KNLA suffered a second major blow which set the resistance forces back fifty years. On 30th January the SPDC assault on Kawmoora, the KNLA's last significant outpost, began. The KNLA and ABSDF stationed 1,000 troops in the base, facing over 1,500 Burma Army soldiers. Round-the-clock shelling slowly decimated the camp and on 21st February, the KNLA and their allies left Kawmoora. They were left with a few thousand guerrillas and little pockets of land in Kawthoolei. "The writing really was on the wall for the Karen," wrote Christian Goodden.[7]

Despite all this suffering and division, the Christian Karens held firm to their faith. The commander of Kawmoora, Colonel Taou Lo, a devout Christian, would stay in contact on his two-way radio with the grieving families of his soldiers who died in the battle. He would pray with them over the radio, and each morning and evening he held Bible study sessions with his soldiers. Some months before the attack, he had had a dream in which he saw an elderly man in a long white robe, with flowing hair. The man's hands were raised in front of him – on his left hand was written the number 16, on his right the number 85, and above his head the number 101. He had this same dream twice, and so discussed it with friends and with his pastor. After praying about it, they all felt that these represented Scriptures in some way. Since the only book in the Bible with either 101 verses or chapters is Psalms, they turned to the Book of Psalms. First, he looked at Psalm 16. "Keep me safe, O God, for in you I take refuge," it began. Psalm 85 verse 4 says: "Restore us again, O God our Saviour, and put away your displeasure towards us." And Psalm 101 starts with: "I will sing of your love and justice; to you, O Lord." Colonel Taou Lo posted these and other Scriptures on the walls of his bunker, and named his battalion "101".[8]

Dr Panter visited the Colonel's wife in the midst of some of the heaviest fighting. Morale was still high despite many casualties. The Karen had intercepted a conversation on the Burmese radio between the artillery officers and the commander in charge of the operation. They were complaining that despite using over 40,000 artillery shells, the land forces had still not been able to capture Kawmoora. As they sat in the Colonel's house, they tried to reach him on the two-way radio to pray for him, but the artillery barrage was too heavy and they could not get through. So instead they prayed together for the Colonel and his men on the battlefield. As the doctor left the house, Colonel Taou Lo's 20-year-old daughter Saleh thanked him for his prayers, and turned to wipe away tears from her face. The Colonel's wife held Dr Panter's hand in hers and said: "It's as if Jesus Christ has come to our home tonight." The doctor was embarrassed, but encouraged. "I trembled at such a comment, knowing full well the multitude of shortcomings of my own life, and my failure to measure up to anything like that which my Lord would require," he wrote in his report. "Yet on reflection I rejoiced that somehow, in some small way we had been able to represent the love of Jesus to them at that time and stand with them in solidarity in this their darkest hour."[9]

Major Mary On was active in these events too, and was a great force for peace and unity. As the commander of Wang Ka camp, she was responsible for 5,000 people, with many Buddhists, Animists and even Muslims living alongside the Christians. Asked how she could maintain harmony in the camp, she replied simply: "I love them. I love them. I love them!" getting louder each time.[10] "How can they resist that? Anyway, we are all Karens, we breathe the same air, eat the same rice, feel the same rain. As Christians we must be an example of Christ's love to them."

As an example of her love for them, during the battle for Kawmoora she, at the age of 61, had run across the battle zone under a hail of enemy gunfire in order to take medicine, gifts and encouragement to the Karen soldiers in the front line. The soldiers at Kawmoora, she said, had no antibiotics because the medical non-governmental organisations (NGOs), such as Medicins sans Frontiers, would not provide aid to military personnel. The troops only had rice and chillies available. During offensives they could not even cook rice because they would have to come above ground to do so. Dr Panter responded to this need by taking her to the nearest town to buy dry food rations which did not require preparation, and two thousand paracetamol tablets, as well as cotton wool and spirits for treating simple wounds.[11]

Other Karen expressed their faith boldly at this time of need. Mr Dun, for example, who had lost all his possessions except the clothes on his back, said: "We are being pruned by the Lord. From a human perspective things do look grim at present. But if we humble ourselves and repent, maybe the Lord will restore us in His good time."[12] Saw Joshua, asked if he felt bitter, laughed: "How could we ever be bitter to the Lord after all He has done for us? No we are thankful for His goodness and pray that we will learn whatever lessons He has for us in this present situation. Perhaps in time if we truly repent He will restore us."[13]

The faith of the Karen Christians is inspiring. But it is important also to remember that the effort to portray the Karen resistance as a Christian struggle against Buddhists comes from the junta itself, and that there are many Buddhist Karen who have remained loyal to the cause. Mahn Sha, the General Secretary of the KNU, is a Buddhist and he emphasises the need to focus on the political struggle for freedom and self-determination. "Some people say it is a Christian revolution, but it is not. There are many Buddhists in the KNU. It is very wrong to say it is a Christian revolution – it is only a Karen revolution," he argued. "The DKBA problem came from the military regime. It was created by the SPDC. They are trying to divide our revolution."

If the Karens are to achieve their desired goal of freedom, they cannot afford another split. They have split over communism, and allowed a situation to develop which caused a religious split. There are concerns now that the definition of the cause itself could create another split. In 2000 Bo Mya was persuaded to step down as President of the KNU, but retained the post of Minister of Defence and was appointed Vice-President. His successor, Saw Ba Thin Sein, perceives the struggle in somewhat different terms to the way Bo Mya saw it.

Bo Mya is a hardline Karen nationalist, for whom it is a fight for a Karen homeland. Ba Thin is a modernist, who recognises that Karen independence is unrealistic and who frames the cause in terms of the wider struggle for democracy and equality in Burma. For Ba Thin, armed struggle alone will not be successful. "Simply fighting will not work. It is a political problem. It is impossible to win the war by armed struggle alone. We struggle for freedom, equal rights, the right of self-determination, and to establish a federal system suitable for a country like Burma. What we need is peace, peace with justice, equal rights, based on democracy."

Asked how the Karen can avoid further divisions, Ba Thin said that they need education. "To be a free nation, to gain freedom, people need to be aware of the situation politically. At the moment illiteracy is very high and there are very few intellectuals among the Karen. We need to know about Burma, about Burman people, and about how to gain their sympathy and understanding."

Bo Mya, however, does not see it that way. There have been splits in the past, and there is the possibility of future splits, he said. "Most people understand that our struggle is for the Karen nation," he argued. "But some people think that if democracy comes to Burma, it will all be well for the Karen people. That is not the case. When democracy comes, we will still have to work for the Karen cause. There are different ideas, different ideologies. It is a question of whether this is a fight for democracy or a fight for Karen freedom. For me, this is an armed struggle for Karen freedom."

While Bo Mya did not name Ba Thin, his views were in stark contrast to those expressed by his successor. Healthy political disagreement is to be expected, but in a resistance struggle unity is essential. The Karen need prayer, not only for their survival but also for their unity, for the two are interdependent.

NOTES

1 Christian Goodden, *Three Pagodas: A Journey Down the Thai–Burmese Border*, p. 242
2 Christian Solidarity Worldwide, Visit to the Thai-Burmese Border, February 6th–10th, 1995
3 Ibid.
4 Ibid.
5 Goodden, p. 242
6 CSW report, February 6th–10th, 1995
7 Christian Goodden, p. 282
8 Ibid.
9 Ibid.
10 Ibid.
11 Ibid.
12 Ibid.
13 Ibid.

CHAPTER SIX

DISPLACED, BUT NOT MISPLACED

"Do not let your hearts be troubled. Trust in God; trust also
in me.
In my Father's house are many rooms.
If it were not so, I would have told you.
I am going there to prepare a place for you."
John 14: 1–2

Ma Nu Kai was fourteen years old, but when I first met her she looked just half that age. Thin and emaciated, she weighed just 22 kilos – less than four stone. Her little brother, Ah Bang, was in a similar state. Aged six, his growth is now permanently stunted. Both children were suffering malnutrition and chronic anaemia. They had been on the run all their lives, and were living in a temporary village close to a KNLA base just inside Karen State. I crossed the border from Thailand to meet them.

Another man, O Thee, has been on the run for fifteen years. He had to flee his home town, in the 7th Brigade area near Pa'an, 20 kilometres away, when the SPDC attacked and has not been able to go back. He has moved from village to village, sometimes living in temporary bamboo homes and sometimes sleeping in the jungle. He told me he had no connection at all with the Karen resistance, but was being pursued purely because he is Karen – which gives the lie to the regime's claim that it only attacks the armed "insurgents".

The village was rife with malaria. Few of the people had mosquito nets or mats to sleep on, and the children only had one T-shirt each. It was suggested to me that if the children even had just one spare set of clothes, that would go a long way towards improving hygiene and ultimately their health. Immediately I was able to provide funds to buy three T-shirts for each of the 35 children in the village. Someone else was able to provide mosquito nets.

I walked around the village. It was much worse than the refugee camps on the Thai side, but these people were still more fortunate than some of the other million or more "internally displaced people" or "IDPs" in Burma. For at least they were close to the border, and they had KNLA soldiers nearby to protect them. Hundreds of thousands live in the jungles, with no food, shelter, medicine or protection, living in constant fear of the military which pursues them.

As I surveyed the conditions – the fear, the disease, the poverty – I felt a sense of despair and hopelessness. I said a prayer. A few minutes later I passed a hut and something inside caught my eye. To my amazement, hanging on the back of the wall with words in English was a banner which destroyed my hopelessness, gave me inspiration and provides a challenge for us all. It asked a very simple question, a question the people of Burma want the world to answer: "Are you for democracy or dictatorship?"

That is the question all of us in the free world need to ask ourselves. For if we are for democracy, why do we tolerate situations like Burma, where democracy is suppressed and over a million people in the eastern regions, and perhaps as many as two million in the country as a whole, are displaced? Of these, over 300,000 are Karens.

In addition to the IDPs trapped behind Burma's borders, there are at least 130,000 Karen and Karenni refugees in camps in Thailand, 50,000 Chin in India and 20,000 Arakanese in Bangladesh.

The situation has escalated in recent years. In 1984, there were only 10,000 Karen refugees in Thailand. In central Dooplaya district of Karen State alone, between April and June 2002, over 5,000 Karens were displaced. In Karenni State, there are estimated to be over 50,000 IDPs and 6,850 held in relocation – or "concentration" – camps.

These hundreds of thousands of people have fled, because to stay means certain death or capture for forced labour. The Burma Army has a crude way of telling people they are to be relocated or taken for forced labour. Often they send their message in the form of a chilli bean, a lump of charcoal or a bullet, in an envelope. The charcoal means the village will be burned down, the bullet signifies that anyone found in the village when the troops come will be shot, and the chilli bean means they will be tortured.

Since 1997, the SPDC has been carrying out an intensive campaign to consolidate its control of the "rugged hills and river valleys of Papun and Nyaunglebin districts in northern Karen State and eastern Pegu Division".[1] The civilian population, not just the armed resistance, has been targeted. Over 200 villages have been destroyed, over 40 SPDC battalions sent in, new roads have been established, and villagers under their control are used for forced labour. Villagers are forbidden to work in their fields, and therefore they lose their rice harvest. Crops and food supplies are destroyed. One IDP, a man named Myo Nyunt from Dweh Loh Township, summed up the situation: "All of us fled with the cats and insects. If we didn't flee like this, then they would have killed everything when they saw it. Only the cockroaches didn't flee."[2]

The life the IDPs live is precarious in the extreme. "We have to find food in the jungle and sometimes we buy it from the rich people. We don't have medicine to treat the sick," said

Saw Thay Doh, originally from Shwegyin Township.[3] "There is no one coming to sell it here. We just stay in the jungle and treat them with bitter gourd leaves. Sometimes we eat boiled rice soup. When our children cry, we have to close their mouths because the Burmese [Army] are staying close to us. We are living like wild birds and chickens. We don't have huts and fences. We make roofs from leaves to keep the ground dry."

Saw Pleh Wah, from Hsaw Tee Township, explained that his people stay in the jungle because otherwise they would be killed. The Burma Army, he said, "treat the civilians just like their enemies. They will kill all the Karen, every man or woman, every time they come into the mountains. For the children they will kill them all, even the little babies who are still drinking from their mother's breasts."[4]

The IDPs report horrific torture when Burma Army troops enter villages. Saw Plaw Doh, from Kyauk Kyi Township, claimed that he had witnessed the shooting of one man, Maung Dta, when the soldiers attacked the village. "After they killed him, they mutilated his body. They took out his liver and intestines, and cut off his penis and testicles," he said. This incident happened on 4th January, 2000.[5]

The Tatmadaw established a terror squad called the "Sa Sa Sa", sometimes known as the "Sa Thon Lon" or "Baw Bi Doh", meaning "short pants soldiers", to carry out the worst atrocities. The Sa Sa Sa is under the direct control of General Khin Nyunt, the first secretary of the SPDC, and it specialises in beheading villagers and putting their heads on display at the entrance to a village as a warning to others. In one incident, Sa Sa Sa troops led by a soldier named Shan Pu fired on a group of young people playing volleyball. They took one young man, cut his head off, stuck a cheroot in his mouth and put the head on display.[6]

Christian villages have been forced by the Sa Sa Sa to pay for the construction of Buddhist temples and help with the labour. The first thing the Sa Sa Sa does when entering a village is to order the villagers to kill all the dogs – thus enabling them to attack at night undetected by barking dogs. "The Sa Thon Lon prefers to stab or slit the throats of their victims rather than shoot them," claims the Karen Human Rights Group.[7]

Forced labour is common in Burma and it is one of the reasons people flee their villages when the Burma Army comes. Those who do not manage to escape are taken to be porters for the military or forced to work on construction projects – and pay for them. Between 1997 and 2002, the Burma Army has extorted over 50 million kyat (US$50,000) from Karens in one township alone, for a road building project. The road is 50 kilometres long and runs alongside military-controlled relocation camps. The Karens, in addition to paying for the road which benefits no one except the military, are also forced to work up to four days a week on building the road, and therefore are unable to attend to their fields and other means of support. As Saw Takkaw says, "Tragically these villagers are forced to facilitate their own oppression."[8]

In 2002, I made one of my crossings into Burma, and met a fifteen-year-old Shan boy. "Tell the world to put pressure on the military regime to stop killing its people," the boy said pleadingly. "Tell the world not to forget us." His appeal was heartfelt and his eyes betrayed his torment as he recounted seeing his father shot dead by Burmese soldiers in his rice paddy.

He had been in his village one day and his father was working in the nearby paddy field. As if out of nowhere, Burma Army soldiers arrived and, with no provocation and for no reason, killed the man as he quietly worked in his paddy. The boy witnessed this, but waited until the military had left the village. Then he went down to the paddy and brought his father's corpse back home for burial.

Two weeks later the Burma Army struck again, this time killing his mother. The village was burned down and he himself was captured and taken as a porter for the military. He was forced to carry heavy loads and walk long distances for three days, with no food or water.

When he collapsed from exhaustion, the soldiers beat him savagely with sticks and guns until he fell unconscious. When he woke up, the soldiers had left and he made his escape. For two weeks he lived in the jungle, eating tree bark and banana pulp. Finally, he made it to the relative safety of a Shan resistance army base.

In addition to forced labour, the Burma Army uses rape as a weapon of war. A report by the Shan Women's Action Network (SWAN) and the Shan Human Rights Foundation, called *Licence to Rape*,[9] documents 625 rapes which took place in Shan State between 1996 and 2001. The population of Shan State makes up 16 per cent of Burma's total population. Some rape victims were as young as five years old. According to the report, 83 per cent of these rapes were perpetrated by officers, often in front of their troops; 61 per cent were gang rapes and 25 per cent of the victims were killed afterwards, their mutilated bodies hung in villages as a warning to others. Some women were taken prisoner by the military and used as sex slaves for soldiers.

These reports have been confirmed by other human rights organisations, and by the US State Department's Bureau of Democracy, Human Rights and Labor. And rape is used well beyond Shan State. In Karen areas it is widespread, but for cultural reasons Karen women are particularly reluctant to tell their story. That does not mean it is not happening in Kawthoolei.

Nan Ei, aged 22, went out looking for dockfruit one day. As she strolled through the jungle, she ran into Burma Army column commander Captain Ye Htut and second-in-command Lieutenant Htin Kyaw. The soldiers took the young woman and her companion to their base and, on 10th June, 2002, twenty soldiers gang-raped her. "I was raped by the column commander, Captain Ye Htut, first, then he ordered his soldiers to rape me," she said the next day. "He said, 'You must all rape that Karen woman. Those who refuse to rape will be shot and killed.'" The next day Nan Ei killed herself.[10]

Thay Yu experienced the same brutality. A Karen mother in her forties, she was fleeing to Thailand because of the oppression by the military in her village. But before she could get to the border, six Tatmadaw soldiers caught one of the families travelling with her. It was a family of four. Thay Yu hid in a bush. She saw the soldiers kill the family's baby with a blow to the back of the neck. Then they raped the mother while forcing the husband to watch. After killing the mother by stabbing her through her vagina with a bamboo pole, they shot the husband. The six-year-old daughter managed to run away.[11]

Rape is the most brutal form of oppression, but there are other, less violent but just as sinister, tactics used by the Burma Army. There are reports that Burma Army soldiers are encouraged to marry ethnic women, in an effort to "dilute" the ethnicity and culture. In Karenni State Burman soldiers are offered a bag of rice worth 6,000 kyats if they marry a Karenni Christian woman,[12] and in Shan and Karen areas it is believed, according to Burma Issues, that "a military policy . . . stipulates an order by which Burmese soldiers are told to marry ethnic women . . . Soldiers that marry an ethnic girl would be rewarded, as these ethnic people 'would only destroy Burma'. They are not Burma nationals and therefore were to be oppressed until they all disappeared from Burma . . . The obvious intention being that if killing and guns can't get rid of them then breeding them out will. Not only would it physically dilute the ethnic races into oblivion but it would also succeed in eradicating the culture and identity of the ethnic groups."[13]

But amidst this darkness are a few beams of light. One such cause for hope is a Karen pastor who devotes his life to helping the IDPs deep inside Burma. For his own safety he cannot be named. But he is a pastor who believes that the most important thing in life is love, and recognises that it is too rarely given. "We talk about love, we know we need love, but we don't give love," he explains.

The pastor studied in a Baptist high school and then a seminary in Burma, and worked in Burma for four years before he decided to return to the border areas to help his people. Perhaps his biggest asset was that he was not an outsider – his own father had been killed and his mother, five months pregnant at the time, had been forced to flee into the jungle. So he knew what it was to be an IDP.

But he also knew that what IDPs need just as much as food and medicine is spiritual support. "I wanted to lead my people. My mother told me that many leaders give their lives for their people, but where are their spirits? So I decided to help my people physically, but also spiritually."

Having studied in a seminary, the pastor felt called to go to the jungles. "I was in the city and I liked the comfort. I did not want to go to the jungle. But I knew that many of our people were there," he said. His first step was to build a school in a village, and work with villagers on developing agriculture and plantation work. Then in 1984, he went to the resistance areas. There he encountered problems.

"They thought I was military intelligence because I spoke Burmese very well and not Karen," he recalls. "People did not trust me. So I just prayed and prayed. They told me they did not like the Christian way and did not believe in their teachers, because the teachers tended to come only for a few months and then they left. I prayed. I wanted to go back to the city but I knew God had called me to my people."

Two months after arriving in the resistance areas, the pastor had a vision. "God told me I was to be a servant not a leader. I was to serve the villagers," he said. He had to change his approach. "Once I realised I was there to be a servant, after three months the villagers' attitude towards me changed. They loved me. Students came to live with me."

Just as he was beginning to establish relationships and his mission in the village, terror struck. The Burma Army attacked and the people dispersed. He fled into the jungle. When the Burmese soldiers left, he returned and started again. He built a new church and school from scratch. Two years on, the military launched another assault. Again the people fled to the jungle, but this time he became separated from his wife and children. He did not know where they had gone. After five days, he found his wife and children sheltering under some trees. They told him they wanted to go home to the city – they did not like the jungle.

He could have done what his family wanted. Or he could have escaped with the flood of refugees to Thailand. But, he said, "there were so many people displaced inside and they were a flock without a shepherd". He stayed with the people, and then moved to the border areas to establish a more secure base for his work and his family.

His next venture was to train others. He started with two or three students, and prepared them for his dangerous mission work. After two years' training, they were sent into the conflict zones.

In 1997 the whole situation for the Karen escalated terribly. Thousands flooded into Thailand and some sought United Nations refugee status and went abroad. "I was very foolish. I decided to stay in the jungle," he said with a smile. But he admitted the struggle he faced personally. "I was having to choose between my family and my people. I tried to help but I couldn't see any results. I thought it was a waste of time being in the jungle, but I prayed and God said 'Don't move'.

I told my wife that I stand for my people, I will help them, but not in a human way, not with an organisation, but in God's way. We had no salary but, by the grace of God, we had food, and my wife agreed for me to carry on."

At this point, however, the pastor became deeply concerned about the material needs of his people. "I wanted to help them but I had no material support to give," he recalls. "I could only give preaching and encouragement. I saw many villages with no blankets or food, and I thought: 'We only preach and encourage, we only give them air, no materials.' I prayed. God opened the door."

He met a foreign missionary, known by his Karen name "Tha-U-Wah-A-Pah", who invited the pastor to accompany him on a trip to the IDPs. "I had not used English for 20 years and never had contact with the outside world, but now a white man was interested in me, by the grace of God. He provided some financial help, and he shared my vision: to provide both physical and spiritual support to the IDPs."

To encourage the IDPs, the pastor started to prepare letters and brochures to send to them, to let them know that they were not forgotten. These brochures simply told the people that they were not alone, that people around the world were praying for them, but that the Karen people needed to stay united.

Sometimes his visits have consequences for the people. "There are many eyes in the jungle," he said. In 2000, he visited a village, and soon after he had left, the Burma Army came and tortured the villagers. But despite that, he tries to follow Jesus' command to love your enemy.

"I didn't want to love the Burmans, but the Bible tells us to. And many Burmese soldiers are innocent – they are simply under orders – and so we need to try to love the people who need love."

On one visit to the IDP areas, he sent a letter to the Burmese soldiers.

"Friends – I know your situation. I love you. Maybe now you feel alone. Maybe now you want to go home. Don't be anxious or afraid, because God loves you." He quoted Isaiah 54:4 and Psalm 118:8–9, and some other scriptures, and concluded with: "We pray for your government, for wisdom for your government, for peace of mind and love and hope for your leaders."

Some SPDC soldiers have defected. They have had enough of killing and hatred and so they run away. Two young soldiers, for example, fled the Tatmadaw in 2001. They said they could no longer tolerate being forced to beat ill and frail elderly people taken for forced labour. They had been ordered to kill the old people who were unable to carry their 30 kilogramme loads – and that was the final straw. They ran away to the Karen camps on the border.[14]

There are exceptions to the brutality of the Burma Army. A Chin soldier, Major Thawng Za Lian, defected in 1999 when he found he was unable to be promoted because he was a Christian. But even though he had served in the Tatmadaw, he had been a rare light in a dark place. When ordered to kill Karen for working in the resistance, instead he went to them and advised them to go to the refugee camps in Thailand. "There are orders to kill you," he told them. "If I am not here, another soldier may come and kill you. So go to the camps."

Another source of help and hope for the IDPs is Dr Cynthia Maung and her backpack medics. Described by the regime as an "absconder, an insurgent and an opium-smuggling terrorist" – and any attempt to deny this, the regime says, is "as futile as covering the rotting carcass of an elephant with a goat hide"[15] – Dr Cynthia is the 43-year-old founder of the Mae Tao Clinic in Mae Sot.

A Karen Christian born in Rangoon, she joined the students fleeing to the Thai border in 1988, providing them with desperately needed medical care. "Traveling at night to evade army hit squads, Maung and 14 colleagues trekked through the jungle for seven days, stopping only to treat the sick and injured they came across with the few supplies they had carried," writes Andrew Marshall in his summary of "Asian Heroes 2003" for *Time* magazine.[16]

Having reached the border, she set about establishing health care for the thousands of refugees. "Equipped with medicines scrounged from foreign relief workers and instruments she had sterilised in a rice cooker, she transformed a dilapidated barn in Mae Sot into a clinic to provide free treatment for the sick and wounded fleeing Burma's oppressive regime," according to Marshall.[17] While she herself, after fifteen years, still has no official papers and is effectively stateless, she is the recipient of numerous international awards in recognition of her work. Today her clinic has five doctors and over a hundred other medical staff, treating over 200 patients a day. In addition, she has 70 teams of backpack medics who go into the conflict zones in Burma, providing treatment for the sick and wounded IDPs and villagers.

The refugees in Thailand are much better off than the IDPs and the soldiers, but their lives are not comfortable either. They live in camps around Mae Sot, Mae Hong Son and Sangkhlaburi, the biggest of which is Mae La Camp. A few are able, with special permission, to live in the towns of Mae Sot and Mae Hong Son, but their existence is precarious – and to make it there, they have had to take an arduous and dangerous route.

Dr Po Thaw Da, the Karen Health Minister, for example, escaped to Thailand from the Burma–India border, with three children and his wife in tow. His journey included a day's truck ride, a day by boat, and several days' walking, pursued by the Burma Army the whole time. Even up until the last few hours of the journey, the Burma Army was tailing him, and he and his wife had to split up and walk through the jungle separately.

Lydia Tamlawah and her husband came to the border in 1980, giving up a job as a teacher at St John's Boys' School in Rangoon, which she had held for 16 years. "We spent three years praying about coming to the border," Lydia told me. "Finally we decided to go. Early one morning, at one o'clock, a friend came with a car and took us to the railway station. We went to Moulmein. Then after several days' journey, we came to the border." They had a hazardous trek from Moulmein to the border, dodging the military intelligence as well as bandits and robbers along the way. Her husband had hidden some maps sewn into a travel mat, and when they got onto a boat for part of the way, a Burma Army officer checked each passenger's belongings. "He eyed the mat. My heart was pumping and I prayed. Thank the Lord, he did not open it," said Lydia. "Then we had to climb up and down the mountains to get to Thailand. We climbed three or four mountains, and slept on the mountainside for a few nights."

While the refugees are relatively safe in comparison with the IDPs, they are not completely safe. The Burma Army and the DKBA have made forays into Thailand to attack the camps.

In January 1996 the DKBA came into Mae La and kidnapped a Karen district chairman. They wanted him to change sides and become a DKBA leader, but he refused. They handed him over to the SPDC and he spent a few years in jail, before escaping, becoming a monk and returning to the border. He is now a member of the KNU Central Committee.

On another incursion, the DKBA killed General Taru, a Karen leader living in the refugee camp. They had wanted to kidnap him, but he was paralysed, so they shot him.

In February, they targeted three refugee camps – Mae La, Waybo and Huay Kaloke, also known as Wang Ka. The DKBA torched the houses and because of the proximity of each house to the other, whole rows of homes – 16 in all in Mae La Camp – were destroyed. They then ran away and mortars and shells from the SPDC followed. Two elderly people were killed, and three children were injured.

Strangely, the Thais made no attempt to defend their territory – for even though the refugees were not Thai, the land was. Since the Thais would make no response, a Karen pastor, the Reverend Dr Simon, decided he would – spiritually. He gathered his students and held a prayer meeting, after having dispatched his wife and young children, and three Naga volunteers, to a safer location. "We prayed 'God, these are your created beings. You can do whatever you like to them,'" he said. "When the shooting started I felt cold and fearful, but after praying, I felt warm, and all fear disappeared."

When Wang Ka Camp, just inside Thailand two kilometres from the KNLA base at Kawmoora, across the border, was hit by shells aimed at Kawmoora, the Karen Health Minister Dr Po Thaw Da was lying on his mat underneath a mosquito net. He got no sleep that night for all around him were exploding shells. For three days, at least 40,000 shells rained down on the troops in Kawmoora and on the camp in Thailand.

Dr Martin Panter was in Wang Ka Camp when the attack took place. "The air was filled with the thunder of exploding shells, plumes of smoke arising from where they fell," he said. "At night the sky was lit up and the fragile bamboo dwellings constructed to house 5,000 Karen refugees in the camp shook with the retort of shells exploding nearby. Little children cried out in fear, to be comforted in turn by their fearful parents. I lay awake on my bed mat, under the mosquito net watching the flashes in the sky, wondering about the madness of such an offensive."[18]

Lydia Tamlawah was in Maesot at the time. "The houses in Maesot shook. Hundreds of mortars were pounding down on Wang Ka every day. People thought that there would be no more Karen people alive," she said. "But the next day, by a miracle, many were still alive."

While the Thais have provided land for sanctuary for the fleeing Karens, in recent years Thailand has tightened its controls over the refugee camps and the border itself. In some cases, the Thai Army has deported Karens fleeing persecution.

On 25th October, 2001, for example, fifteen families – totalling 63 people – fled to Thailand having escaped a Burma Army-controlled forced relocation centre. They were pursued for five days by 300 Burmese soldiers and had spent two weeks hiding in thick jungle. According to Saw Takkaw, a human rights worker who heard about the case: "The group then decided that the only way for them to survive was to flee to Thailand. They were in no condition for such a long and dangerous journey, but there was no choice. Burmese soldiers were searching for them in the area, and Saw SS, who suffered from a gunshot wound to the arm, would not be able to hold out much longer without medical treatment. And so the decision was made: the 63, a band of scared and exhausted civilians, would make a daring run to the border. Saw SS was placed in a makeshift stretcher and sent ahead of the group."[19]

The conditions were terrible. There were heavy rains and the terrain was rugged. While this had the advantage of enabling them to slip by within earshot of the Burmese troops, "the arduous journey to perceived salvation in Thailand came with a price". One old lady died from diarrhoea, others suffered from malaria, leeches, hunger and exhaustion.[20] Finally, however, they made it to the supposed safety of Thailand.

Within a few days, however, their fate changed. The Thai Army caught them and on 6th November, Thai soldiers loaded them up on trucks. They were told they were being taken to Tonya Refugee Camp in Sangklaburi – but this was actually a lie. Even the intervention of the border police did not help. The police told the Thai 9th Army that to deport these people would be inhumane, but the military refused to listen.

Officially, the group was sent across the border to Hteewadoh, a Mon village. But this too was untrue. They were in fact sent to Halawkani, according to Saw Takkaw. Halawkani is a Mon refugee camp inside Burma. Since the Mon have a ceasefire with the SPDC, they were nervous about sheltering Karen escapees and so they rejected them. The group had to walk to Htweewadoh. But here, too, the Mon were reluctant to help, fearing it could provoke an SPDC attack. Their fears were well-founded, and the Mon-SPDC ceasefire broke down shortly after this incident.

On 20th November at 7 a.m, the Burmese troops attacked Hteewadoh and burned the whole village. Fortunately most of the 63 had already fled to Peh Toh Weh. Pursued by the Burma Army, they moved on deeper inside a "black zone" with a heavy military presence, where they remain today.

Their deportation was confirmed by Major-General Mana Prajakit, commander of the 9th Infantry Division of the Thai Army. He said publicly that "63 Burmese immigrants seeking refugee status in Thailand were forcibly sent home".[21]

One of the Karens involved in this case summed up their situation with this analogy: "IDPs are like chickens in a cage. Whenever the master wants to eat one of them, he can do it easily. If the chicken runs or stands still, it does not matter. He will still die."

Nevertheless, many of the refugees, despite the restrictions and the insecurity, have shown remarkable resourcefulness in making the most of the opportunities that the comparative safety of Thailand gives them. In Umpiem Camp, Saw Stephen has started a school which now educates 1,600 refugee children. The school has 55 teachers, all unpaid volunteers, and they teach Karen, Burmese, English, Thai, physics, chemistry, world history, geography and mathematics. Saw Stephen, who was born near Rangoon in 1932, is also a deacon of the church.

The Karen people are full of colourful characters, and in Umpiem Camp there are many. Most have either Karen names or traditional English names, but one particular family is very unusual. The eldest son is a pastor, and his name is Billy Graham. The second son, a musician and worship leader, is Billy Sunday. The third is Marvelous Jerry but is generally just known as Marvelous. And the last son – believe it or not – goes by the name of Guacamole. The parents, who are elderly, use the Karen terms for "Grandpa" – Poo Poo – and "Grandma" – Pee Pee.

In one camp I was walking along and a little boy came up to me with his mother. "My name is Winston Churchill," he said. I laughed, but it turned out to be his real name. A man who works with the Karen education department in Maesariang is called Saw Wingate, after the British soldier.

Meredith Nunu is yet another inspiring example of courage and faith. She is a Karenni refugee in one of the camps outside Mae Hong Son, and she had seen her husband shot dead in his rice paddy by the Burma Army. She gathered her children and fled to Thailand.

Meredith did not sit around feeling sorry for herself. She saw that in the refugee camp there were many children without parents. Either their parents were dead or they had become separated from them. So she founded an orphanage and a school to care for the children. Dr Panter, who has helped to support Meredith's work, notes that "the kids are balanced, beautiful and they love one another".

Meredith has instilled a strong Christian culture into her orphanage and school. The children all have an extraordinary ability to recite Scriptures in English, Burmese and Karenni. They have a strict regime – they rise at 4.30 a.m. for an hour of prayer, then they have an hour of chores before breakfast. After school they have two hours of praise and worship. Some foreign visitors have expressed concern at such a rigorous schedule, but the children all seem to be happy and, after all, they are not forced to stay – if they wanted to leave, they could. They all choose to stay.

Hanging on the wall of Meredith's bamboo hut are words from great thinkers. Albert Camus' words proclaim that "the passage from speech to moral action has a name – to become human", and Albert Einstein's stand alongside Camus': "Great spirits have always encountered violent opposition from mediocre minds". But perhaps most inspiring of all are Meredith's own words: "I would be true, for there are those who trust me; I would be humble, for I know my weakness; I would be strong, for there is much to suffer." On the walls of the nursery school are the words of "The Motto Song of the Nursery School of Camp 3":

> For God is our strength,
> In Him we do and dare
> The right against the wrong
> We cherish everywhere
> Here firmly let us stand
> United hearts and hands
> And pray that God
> May bless and keep
> Our nursery school
> Our happy land
> From far and near
> We must to love
> The right to dare
> Our nursery school
> Hold high her name
> Her noble name
> Shall never fail.

Pastor Jolly lives up to his name entirely. A former KNU resistance soldier, he now runs a Bible school. In 1954, he joined the resistance and worked in the Karen police force for a year before joining the Karen commandos. But in 1969, after some years of fighting the armed struggle, he decided to retire and become "a Christian soldier". He started work as an evangelist, and describes himself now as a "Jesus commando". In November 1997 he was ordained as pastor of a charismatic Baptist church, and he founded the Bible school with the aim of sending itinerant evangelists into Burma.

The evangelists who go out from Pastor Jolly's school into Burma each week have to pass between the DKBA and the SPDC to reach the villages. In three years they have built a church and baptised 72 people. But permission to build another church has been refused by the SPDC, who told the evangelists that Burma is a Buddhist country.

The Reverend Dr Simon – sometimes known as Pastor Simon – lives in Mae La Camp. He was born on 19th July, 1949, Martyrs Day in Burma and the day the Karen freedom movement started. Born into a Christian family, he made a personal commitment to Christ when he was living in Kyawchi at the end of his middle school years. "But I did not have a deep understanding of salvation," he admits. "I lived as a nominal Christian."

Then in 1965 he had several dreams which changed the course of his life. "I dreamed that I was flying over mountains, rivers and seas, and I had a peculiar kind of peace. After these dreams I just knew that God was about to do something to change my life," he said. But it was a while before the message of these dreams was revealed.

Pastor Simon was a bright student and a keen athlete. He competed in marathons, and on one occasion he spent two whole days running, competing in the 5,000 metre race, 10,000 metres and a marathon, one after the other. He collapsed from exhaustion at the end, unable to breathe. "I thought I was dying. I prayed for God's healing power. I told

Him that if He healed me, I'd do whatever he wanted," he recalls. "The doctor checked me and concluded that the only thing wrong with me was 'over-exercise'! I had to drink lots of water and have complete rest for a month."

While recuperating, a nurse told the young Simon that she wanted to help people go to Bible school, and wondered if he was interested. He thought perhaps this was God opening a door for him. "I knew this was the answer," he said. He accepted her generosity and went to Burma Divinity School in Rangoon to do a Bachelor of Theology degree. He studied on what was known as "Seminary Hill" – where there were three theological institutes, a Karen, a Burmese and an English institute.

In 1973 he completed his Bachelor's degree and continued his studies for a second degree. He was then appointed to teach in the seminary. He specialised in "Biblical Theology" – studying and teaching the origins of the Bible, particularly the Old Testament. His academic work led to him spending two years in the Philippines from 1985 to 1987 to do a doctoral programme. Little did he know that through this study, God was preparing him to teach theology and lead a church among refugees.

In August 1987 Pastor Simon returned to Burma, and took up a post in the seminary as a professor of theology. A year later the student uprising was in full flow. The University Christian Fellowship in Rangoon became involved, and Pastor Simon was asked by the university authorities to take responsibility for the pastoral care of the students during the crisis. He organised public prayer gatherings.

The situation in Rangoon became so bad that Pastor Simon and his wife decided to leave the capital and go to Karen State. "We could hear shooting all night. There were rumours that the water and food had been poisoned. There was no security. Life was very insecure," he recalls.

To hide the fact that they were fleeing, Pastor Simon and his wife made several trips out of Rangoon prior to their final escape. They went to Pa'an, Tonguoo and Henzada to lead Bible study sessions. Finally they left on what appeared to be just another church trip – but unbeknown to the authorities, they were not to return. They had a hazardous journey across mountains and through rivers, and they could only take a handful of belongings. They were accompanied by thirteen other people, and the group included Pastor Simon's ageing father-in-law, a Karen leader called Johnny Htoo, who had to be carried by four people.

The journey to Manerplaw took more than two months, but finally they arrived and were invited to stay with Saw Ba Thin Sein. Pastor Simon was asked to teach at the Bible school based in Wallay, and after a short time he was elected Principal of the Kawthoolei Karen Bible School and College (KKBSC).

In December 1989, the Burma Army attacked Wallay and Pastor Simon had to move once again. In early 1990 he and his family crossed the border and became refugees. They moved to Mae La Camp.

Not long after arrival in Mae La, Pastor Simon prayed about starting a new Bible school in the refugee camp. He sought and secured the permission of the Karen leaders. He started with four or five teachers from the school in Wallay, and 45 students, in 1990. Over the years since then the school's size and reputation have grown remarkably. Theologians from the Philippines visited and were impressed. The Baptist World Alliance and the Asian Baptist Federation decided to accredit the school, and a Bachelor of Theology programme was added to the syllabus in 1993. In 1996, a Bachelor of Arts course was introduced, offering secular subjects such as political science, history, economy, education and English. In 2002, the school had 233 students and 20 faculty members – all in a refugee camp on the Thai–Burmese border.

In 2000, Pastor Simon's remarkable work was recognised by the Baptist World Alliance when they awarded him their Human Rights Award. This prize was introduced in 1990 and is only offered once every five years. The first winner, in 1995, was former US President Jimmy Carter. He was followed five years later by a refugee pastor from Burma, Pastor Simon.

However, Pastor Simon was not permitted to receive the award from the Baptist World Alliance Congress in Melbourne, Australia. Although a request was made to both the United Nations and the Thais for permission to travel to Australia, the request was turned down. The Thais were concerned that it could set a precedent. They told him if he wanted to go, he could find a country to sponsor him and they would allow him to leave – but he would not be allowed back. "I am here to help and live with my people. So if I went and could not come back, I cannot help my people," Pastor Simon explains. He decided not to go.

When Pastor Simon returned to Burma from his doctoral programme in the Philippines, the authorities forced him to hand over his passport at the airport. When he fled to the border, he left behind his identity card, bank account and driving licence. "It is a little frustrating. I know how to drive, and I have a car now donated by friends from Australia and Thailand, but I have no licence! I can't travel, as I have no passport."

Pastor Simon's writings are a great inspiration to those who meet him. His use of the English language, and the depth of spiritual meaning he puts into the pieces he writes, is remarkable. In one piece, which is a tribute to the faith of the Karen Christians, he writes:

They call us a displaced people,
But praise God; we are not misplaced.
They say they see no hope for our future,

But praise God; our future is as bright as the promises of God.
They say they see the life of our people is a misery,
But praise God; our life is a mystery.
For what they say is what they see,
And what they see is temporal.
But ours is the eternal.
All because we put ourselves
In the hands of the God we trust.

In another similar message, he wrote this:

I am not ashamed to be a refugee, for I know my Lord, my
    Master, my Saviour,
Was a refugee long, long before me.
I am not afraid to be a refugee, for though I am displaced, I am
    not misplaced.
I will never feel lonely, for God gives me many friends around
    the world.
I will never feel helpless, for God gives me many hands for
    help.
I will never stop doing good things in spite of all the difficulties
    and hardships, for
I know that this is the real purpose of life God has entrusted to
    each one of us.
I will never feel regret being a refugee, for though life is full of
    limitations, restrictions and tragedies, it is enriched with
    meanings and values.
I will never feel hopeless, for my Saviour has promised me an
    eternal home.
I am glad to be a refugee for I am always reminded that my
    eternal home is in heaven and not on this earth.
But I know that for the time being, Satan is trying to enslave me,
    for though I live in my Father's, my brothers' and sisters'
    world, I am not free to travel.
However I am strongly convinced that a day will come – and it
    will be soon – that I will be able to travel freely to visit my

brothers and sisters around the world and say "Thank you"
for what they have done.
I will see the beauty of my Father's world. Amen.

Such is the courage and faith of the refugees and IDPs of
Burma, and those among them who serve others. They may be
displaced, but they are undoubtedly not misplaced.

NOTES

1 Karen Human Rights Group (KHRG), *Flight, Hunger and Survival: Repression and Displacement in the Villages of Papun and Nyaunglebin District*, October 2001
2 Ibid.
3 Ibid.
4 Ibid.
5 Ibid.
6 CSW *Response, Licence to Kill in Burma*, June 1999
7 Karen Human Rights Group
8 Saw Takkaw, *63 Lives That Do Not Matter: Persecuted in Burma, Denied Sanctuary in Thailand*, December 2002
9 Shan Women's Action Network and Shan Human Rights Foundation, *Licence to Rape*, published May 2002
10 Lord Clarke of Hampstead, debate on Burma, House of Lords, December 3rd, 2002, *Hansard*
11 Refugees International, Testimony by Veronika Martin, Advocate, to the Senate Committee on Foreign Relations Subcommittee on East Asian and Pacific Affairs, June 18th, 2003
12 Christian Solidarity Worldwide, Visit to the Thai–Burmese border, April 22–May 14, 2003
13 *The Deeper We Probe,* Burma Issues, October 2002
14 Baroness Cox, *Burma: Bombs into Bells*, Prophecy Today, September/October 2001

15 Andrew Marshall, "Dr Cynthia Maung – Healer of Souls", *Time*, 28th April 2003

16 Ibid.

17 Ibid.

18 Christian Solidarity Worldwide report, February 6–10, 1995

19 Saw Takkaw

20 Ibid.

21 Ibid.

CHAPTER SEVEN

LIGHT IN THE DARKNESS

Love each other,
Unite and work for freedom, justice and peace.
Forgive and don't hate each other.
Pray with faith, act with courage, never surrender.
The Free Burma Rangers

It was almost midnight when I returned to the guest house in the border town of Maesot after a long day visiting the Karen refugee camps. As I walked up the steps I bumped into a foreign missionary who works with the internally displaced people deep inside Burma. He risks his life in this work and hence his real name cannot be used. He had named his daughter "Tha-U-Wah", meaning "White Monkey" in Karen, and so, in Karen custom, he became "Tha-U-Wah-A-Pah" or "Father of the White Monkey". He later discovered that the Karen had a legend that claims that when the people are oppressed, a white monkey will come and help them, and so his name had a deeper significance.

"Hey, have you seen *Lord of the Rings*?" Tha-U-Wah-A-Pah asked.

I told him I had.

"Well, it's Burma!"

Instantly I could see the analogy.

"Mordor is the SPDC, and guys like us are hobbits. We're just little guys trying to do some good. On the surface it seems like Mordor has all the strength and power and might. But if our fellowship of hobbits stays united, good will defeat evil in the end." Gandalf's words in *Lord of the Rings* have a particular relevance: "That way lies our hope, where sits our greatest fear. Doom hangs still on a thread. Yet hope there is still, if we can but stand unconquered for a little while."

A few months after that conversation, I found myself walking through dense jungle from Thailand into Shan State, Burma, with Tha-U-Wah-A-Pah and his "Free Burma Rangers": the Black Monkey, the Leopard, the Bird and two Mad Dogs. Only missing were the Koala Bear, the Green Monkey, the Barking Deer and the Vulture. I truly felt like a hobbit. There was the risk of the Thai Army catching us crossing the border, there was the Burma Army not too far away, there were Shan State Army (SSA) resistance soldiers who, although on our side, were said to be unpredictable, and there was the jungle.

We hiked for six hours up and down steep mountainsides, not using pathways but hacking our way through the undergrowth. The soil was so loose and the slopes so steep that it was rather like skiing. I spent much of my time on my backside sliding down the hills. At one point I tripped on a root, and slid head first down the mountain straight towards a large tree. I thought to myself that of all the heroic ways to die in Burma, either at the hands of the Tatmadaw or Khun Sa's drug runners, or on a landmine or by snake bite, brain damage from hitting a tree trunk at full speed would not be high on the list. However, I was uninjured and continued the journey. We walked through streams and clambered over fallen tree trunks. One of my friends, an Australian who was over 60 and reminded us of Gandalf, fell down steep crevices into thick foliage numerous times and almost disappeared.

At one point on this trek the strap of my water bottle broke and I watched as the container – my only source of water for the entire journey – tumbled down the mountainside and disappeared into the jungle. I did not give it a second thought. It is gone and "that's it", I believed. Besides, the over one million internally displaced people have to go for days and nights in the jungle with little water, food or medicine, with heavy loads on their backs, screaming babies in their arms and sweat on their brow from fear of the Burma Army. Given that knowledge, I was not going to fuss over a little water bottle.

However, to my amazement, a few minutes later one of the Karen members of the Free Burma Rangers team, a man known as "the Black Monkey", came running up to me carrying my water bottle. I stared at him in amazement. How on earth he had scrambled down the hill, retrieved my water bottle which to my eyes had been buried in the jungle, and returned it to me all in the space of a few minutes, without even being out of breath was miraculous. But then, he was a Free Burma Ranger.

Tha-U-Wah-A-Pah was born in Thailand, the son of a missionary couple. He returned to his own country to join the military, and served for several years in the special forces. He served in anti-narcotics operations in South America, before working with Thai special forces. Then he got married, and in 1993 left active duty and went to Fuller Seminary in the United States to study for a Master of Divinity degree. He decided to become a missionary.

His missionary work in Burma started with the Wa, an ethnic minority group that had been associated with the Chinese-backed Burmese Communist Party but had broken away. The Wa's Foreign Minister was a Christian and had been dispatched to Thailand to seek outside help.

Tha-U-Wah-A-Pah and his wife were particularly inspired by the example of William Marcus Young, the first missionary to the Wa in the early 1900s. Like the Karen, the Wa's folk religion contained interesting fables with biblical parallels. They believed in prophets, whom they called *Siyeh*, and in the 1880s one such prophet, called Pu Chan by the Shan people, persuaded several thousand Wa tribesmen to give up their practices of headhunting and spirit worship. The true God, Pu Chan told his people, was about to send "a white brother with a copy of the lost book". If the white brother came into the Wa areas and learned about their practices he might turn back.

One day Pu Chan saddled a pony and told the people to follow it. "Siyeh told me last night that the white brother has finally come near! Siyeh will cause this pony to lead you to him. When you find the white brother, let him mount this pony. We would be an ungrateful people if we made him walk the last part of his journey toward us!"[1]

The Wa people followed the pony over 200 miles of mountainous trails to Kengtung. On arrival in the city, the pony turned into the gate of the mission compound and stopped at the well. The people looked all around but could not see a white man. However, what happened next was extraordinary. The people heard some noises from the well and peered inside. There was no water – but instead, two people. "Hello strangers!" said one of them, a white man with a beard. "May I help you?" William Marcus Young climbed out the well. "Have you brought a book of God?" the Wa asked. Young nodded and the people fell at his feet.[2]

Young worked with the Wa and passed on his passion for these people to his descendants. His great grandson, for example, lives in Thailand working with the Wa today. One of the Young family was a friend of Tha-U-Wah-A-Pah's father in Chiang Mai and on his visit to Thailand to seek help, the Wa Foreign Minister visited Tha-U-Wah-A-Pah's father. He saw a photograph of the man's son in military uniform. "A soldier – that's the type of missionary we need," he said.

So in 1993, 1994 and again in 1995 Tha-U-Wah-A-Pah, who was still in seminary, and his wife did three short-term missions to the Wa, leading pastoral training, medical training, village health care and evangelism. They took a trip through China and crossed the border into Wa territory from Kunming. But in 1996, the Wa sent word that the political situation was too sensitive and that they should not come.

On every mission, Tha-U-Wah-A-Pah developed relationships with the Wa Christian Fellowship, and helped to start student hostels, village projects and church work. But in 1996 he faced a crisis of confidence, a time of personal questioning. He missed the military life and wondered whether he was really cut out to be a missionary. He didn't feel like a pastor.

In the midst of this time of searching, Tha-U-Wah-A-Pah went for a run, one of his favourite activities. He and his wife both run marathons, and their daily exercise involves usually at least a seven mile run. On this run, he felt an itch to rejoin the army and doubts about being a missionary, but felt God saying to him "just give thanks" and trust God.

The following day, his sister was visiting Tha-U-Wah-A-Pah and his family in Thailand and she suggested they take a trip to Rangoon. "Let's just go and see the situation there," she said. He had already been blacklisted by the SPDC because of his work with the Wa but, remarkably, succeeded in obtaining a visa.

While in Rangoon, his sister said to Tha-U-Wah-A-Pah: "Let's try to go and see Aung San Suu Kyi."

Never one to miss an opportunity, Tha-U-Wah-A-Pah agreed and they went and knocked on the Burmese democracy leader's front gate. An aide answered the gate and told them to telephone for an appointment. They went back to the hotel and made the call. To their surprise, Daw Suu Kyi agreed to see them.

In their meeting, Daw Suu Kyi, a committed Buddhist, told Tha-U-Wah-A-Pah that she reads the Bible every day. "My favourite verse is 'You will know the truth and the truth will set you free'" (John 8:32). Her mother was a Karen and a Christian who had shared some of her beliefs with Daw Suu Kyi. Tha-U-Wah-A-Pah asked if he could pray, and she said "Yes. I need prayer. Please ask other people to pray for us."

She also said that the Burmans were oppressing the ethnic groups and would continue to oppress them in the future unless something was done. "It is our nature, but it is wrong and I want to change it," she said. "We need unity among the Burmans and the ethnic groups." Tha-U-Wah-A-Pah said he would try to organise a worldwide prayer movement, and help in reconciliation and unity efforts.

Tha-U-Wah-A-Pah's mission was born. He returned to Thailand rejuvenated, with his heart increasingly drawn to the work of uniting the different ethnic nationalities – the Karen, Karenni, Shan, Wa, Chin, Kachin, Arakan, Mon and others – in the struggle for justice and peace. Some of the ethnic groups, such as those on the western border, were harder to reach, but those on the eastern border of Burma, notably the Karen, Karenni, Shan, Mon and Wa, were accessible. For Tha-U-Wah-A-Pah, the will of God for each person is where "the world's greatest need and your deepest desire meet". There was no doubt about the need the ethnic groups, especially those displaced in the jungle, faced, and Tha-U-Wah-A-Pah was certain what his desire was.

The Free Burma Rangers group was born in 1997, during a major offensive by the Burma Army. Tha-U-Wah-A-Pah emphasises that the entire work has been built and driven by God. "I recruited no one. When I started, I knew that it was important to feel that God was the driving force. So I just started moving along and people joined," he explained.

He was inspired by the book *Grandfather Longlegs*, the story of Major Hugh Seagrim. "It is a story about faith, love and sacrifice in the face of great odds," he said. "It inspired me and made me realise that no dictator could stop anyone from loving and serving others. So I decided, along with Htoo Htoo Lay of the KNU, to start the Free Burma Rangers. We would go with whatever we had to give help, hope and love to those suffering under the attacks of the Burma Army."

The first person Tha-U-Wah-A-Pah met was a young Karen man now known as "the Mad Dog". All the team have animal names, partly for security and partly for amusement and comradeship.

In 1997 the KNLA was in total retreat. Their base at Manerplaw had fallen two years previously and their future looked dire. Over 100,000 refugees had fled their homes and crossed the border into Thailand, and there were believed to be over 2 million people internally displaced, with at least a million in eastern Burma alone. Tha-U-Wah-A-Pah went to the border to see what he could do to help. As he got out of his truck, the Mad Dog literally walked straight out of the jungle.

"He was in full combat uniform, had a big earring in one ear, and he looked dashing. He had a wild-man air about him, he looked above the rules, like a pirate," Tha-U-Wah-A-Pah recalls. "He is the son of a pastor, and he's a kickboxing champion, athlete, cook, soldier, artist and medic."

"Hello," the Mad Dog said. "I am a medic and a soldier. How can I help you?"

"I thought he was an angel," says Tha-U-Wah-A-Pah.

Refugees were pouring across the border fleeing the fighting, and so Tha-U-Wah-A-Pah and the Mad Dog got to work.

"We went in with backpacks and treated lots of people. We picked up a guy who had stepped on a landmine, and took him to hospital where his leg was amputated," he said.

But after they had helped as many refugees as possible, the Mad Dog left. "My wife and kids are still somewhere inside Burma. I have to find them," he told Tha-U-Wah-A-Pah.

"In life, you can only do what you can where you are and leave the rest to God," Tha-U-Wah-A-Pah believes.

When he was younger, the Mad Dog wanted to fight the Burmese regime because he had witnessed the atrocities they carried out. He had grown up with the resistance and became a Karen soldier. He was involved in very heavy fighting. But then, he says, "I saw my people suffering, I saw their living conditions and their eating conditions. I saw their health conditions. When I saw the suffering, I wanted to help but I didn't know how," he says. "Then I met Tha-U-Wah-A-Pah."

Earlier, Tha-U-Wah-A-Pah had met Htoo Htoo Lay, the Joint General Secretary of the KNU and a leader of the Committee for Internally Displaced Karen People (CIDKP). Htoo Htoo Lay is the embodiment of generosity, warmth and faith, and has the most remarkable ability to laugh and smile in the face of adversity. His name means "golden golden cliff" – the repetition of "golden" equals "pure gold", he said, and his heart certainly reflects that. A lawyer by training, he left his post as a government law officer and public prosecutor in Burma in 1977 and came to the Thai border. "I had realised that because of so many injustices in the judicial and executive systems, I could not do anything to help the oppressed people inside. That's why I came to the border," he said. He worked for the KNU first as an intelligence officer in the Karen capital Pa'an, before rising to become the KNU Justice Minister, and then Joint General Secretary.

According to Tha-U-Wah-A-Pah, Htoo Htoo Lay walked an extraordinary tightrope in seeking reconciliation between different Karen factions, especially the KNU and the DKBA. He received death threats from both sides at one point. "The amazing thing is he does not pray for protection," Tha-U-

Wah-A-Pah told me. "He prays for God's will to be done, and for him to be in the right place at the right time. He says that God can take him whenever He wants."

Htoo Htoo Lay is also a lay preacher. Born into a Christian family, he was raised as a Baptist but as a teenager he worked with a Pentecostal church. "Because of that background and experience, I became well devoted to the Christian faith," he said. "At university in my spare time I worked as a pastor of a church and as a lay preacher, going here and there, preaching on the roads!"

Tha-U-Wa-A-Pah and Htoo Htoo Lay agreed that they had to do something to help the people – they could not rely on outside help. So they formed the first Free Burma Ranger team, with a soldier, a medic, an assistant medic, a pastor and videographer, a photographer and reporter and a nurse.

Tha-U-Wah-A-Pah's wife recalls one of their first missions, in which her eyes were opened to the generosity of the Karen people. It was a three-week mission to the IDPs, and for the whole trip the people wanted to help Tha-U-Wah-A-Pah and his wife. "They wanted to carry my pack, they offered us food to eat first, they shared snacks, they offered us baths, the best places to sleep, and they just served us constantly," she said. "But we had all walked the same mountains – they were tired too. Their love and generosity was more than I had ever experienced."

Such an approach showed her an alternative view on life. "The gifts they gave were of themselves – their time, energy and love. In my experience in the West it is easier to go to the store and buy a trinket as a gift," she said. "For this reason I have chosen to raise my children in this war. The influence of these people is something I have never experienced anywhere else."

One of the Free Burma Rangers' first contributions to the ethnic struggle in Burma was to facilitate and coordinate the

Mae Tha Raw Hta Ethnic Nationalities Seminar in 1997, aimed at helping the different ethnic nationalities develop leadership and communication skills, and to improve coordination and unity between them. Tha-U-Wah-A-Pah got to know some of the leaders, who invited him to visit their areas. He also invited the organising committee to institute a time of silent prayer at the start of each day of meetings. At the end of the seminar, one leader, who was not a Christian, approached him and said: "Your God was here. We have never had a more peaceful, conciliatory multi-ethnic meeting." Since then, three other unity and reconciliation seminars have been held, resulting in the formation of the Ethnic Nationalities Solidarity Consultation Committee (ENSCC), which works for a resolution to the conflict. A little later, General Bo Mya, the Karen leader, heard of Tha-U-Wah-A-Pah and invited him to a meeting. He asked him whether he sympathised with the Karen. Tha-U-Wah-A-Pah's answer was direct and frank:

"I don't sympathise with them, I love them." He showed the General his hand and pointed at the ring on his finger, given to him by the Mad Dog as a symbol of their bond.

The Mad Dog was followed by "the Bird", who joined the Free Burma Rangers as a Buddhist but later became a Christian as the result of repeated dreams he had been having in which Jesus appeared.

"The Black Monkey" came along next, in 1997, and he was a tricky character. He came from a Christian family and had been baptised in 1985, but he did not have a personal faith, and even challenged the basic Christian concepts. In the 1988 democracy uprising he left home and joined the Karen resistance, serving as a soldier, a teacher and a nurse.

In 1996, the Black Monkey's cousin went to school in Toungoo, and wrote a letter to his parents in which he said: "We miss you, and we are praying for you, and we are praying for knowledge and wisdom." The Black Monkey said he "felt sad that his cousins, who were younger than him, knew how to pray". He decided he wanted to be able to pray with them. He challenged God, saying: "If you are real, prove it. If not, I won't pay any attention to you."

That year he attended a convention organised by the Asia Institute of Christian Communication (AICC), but found it a difficult experience. His English at the time was poor, and he had got into an argument with an "old grandfather" who had pushed the Black Monkey to go to the convention. "I did not want to – I prayed that I could avoid the training," he says. In the end, however, he went to the training, despite the great expense involved, and was encouraged by what he experienced. "Without God I would not have got the chance to go," he admits. Although friends suggested he remain in Thailand to improve his English, he decided to express his gratitude to God through action, and went back to the refugee camps to share what he had learned. He then met Tha-U-Wah-A-Pah, who invited him on a mission to Karenni state. In 1997 he became the "pastor" to the Free Burma Rangers team, and also took on responsibility for videography.

Then came the "Barking Deer". A nurse, she had spent two years in prison in Tavoy and was nearly executed by her own people because they thought she had joined the junta while in jail. She has witnessed terrible atrocities. In 1992, she and her husband were ambushed by the Burma Army. While she managed to flee, she had to abandon her baby son. Her husband was stripped naked, bayoneted and shot through the mouth, and left to die. Yet she is determined to help her people and wants to study to become a doctor.

"I know that when the Burmese soldiers come to an area, even if only one villager is left in the village, they will kill that villager," she said. "We know they are wicked and their hearts are full of evil."[3]

A second "Mad Dog" was a Karenni man who had been – indeed, still was – a soldier. He had killed lots of people and, according to Tha-U-Wah-A-Pah, had a hard heart. When he first encountered the Free Burma Rangers he looked down disparagingly on the idea of "missions". Now, aged 46, he wants to go to Bible school. He is now the team leader, is the most mature and is the guiding hand on all missions. He is just as tough as he ever was, but now uses that tough spirit to endure hardships in order to love and serve others.

Finally there was Doh Say, an official in the Karenni Foreign Office, who was given the animal name "the Vulture". Doh Say had been a soldier with the Karenni National Progressive Party (KNPP). He fled Burma in 1991, and took up arms because, he said, "I wanted to free myself and the Karenni people, and I wanted to take revenge against the Burma Army". But soon after he had gone to the front line, Doh Say was seriously wounded in combat, shot in his back and stomach. It took him two years to recover, and so in 1995 he turned to political work as a means of continuing the struggle.

Like others in the Free Burma Rangers, Doh Say came from a Christian family. He is Karen, but grew up in Karenni State. His faith only came alive, however, when his life hung in the balance. Until he was wounded in battle, he had, he recalls, only prayed when he was in trouble. But in 1992 he went to the front line and stayed there for ten days. He recalled a story of a captain who went to the front line with Psalm 23 in his pocket. Although the captain was shot, his life was saved. So Doh Say took Psalm 23 too. But, he thought, what happens if a bullet hits one of the other pockets? He got caught up in some of the heaviest shelling of the conflict, and at three o'clock in the afternoon of the fourth day of fighting, he was hit. He stumbled and fell down a cliff. Hanging on the edge of the rockface, trying to cling on to the cliff as well as his life, Doh Say closed his eyes. Blaming God in anger, he believed his time had come.

A few days later Doh Say woke up in hospital. But for weeks he suffered flashbacks. The sound of gunfire kept ringing in his ears. Slowly, however, he started to recover. He also started to trust God for the first time.

"My faith is growing, becoming stronger," he says now. "I have no skills but I believe God has something for me. He gave me a chance to be His child."

Some aspects of faith still present a challenge to Doh Say, as they do for every Christian. "The Bible teaches us to pray for our enemies, but it is difficult," he admits. "When I was a student, my teacher told us to love each other and to love our enemies. But in practice it is very difficult. Up to now I haven't implemented this yet!"

But through his experiences of God, Doh Say says his attitude towards prayer has changed. "Now I find I cannot go to sleep without praying first, even in normal times. In peaceful times, I still remember God. I ask God not to lead me into temptation. But before I never felt like that," he explains. "Now if I don't pray, I worry. But if I pray, I don't worry."

Doh Say is confident that one day, the dictatorship in Burma will fall. "We must trust God. With his help, and with unity and co-operation, definitely the situation will change. Dictatorships can never last. One day they will fall down," he believes. "Maybe today we are militarily losing. But it's not the end yet. In the end, the evil dictatorship will lose."

In his most profound expression of faith, Doh Say articulated what the other Free Burma Rangers, and many people struggling for freedom in Burma, believe. "I am not afraid to die," he said. "My objective is to enter the Kingdom of God. My objective is not to get this or that, a big house or become a millionaire. My objective is to serve God."

After the terrorist attacks in Washington DC and New York on 11th September, 2001, Doh Say wrote a message to his international friends from his refugee home on the Thai–Burmese border. He said that he was "traumatised" and deeply saddened by the terrorist attacks. "I was about to cry when I saw the people who were waving for help . . . I saw their faces before they were killed . . . I wish I was there and could do just whatever I could. From here I feel very useless. But what can I do from here? Nothing but I pray for everyone who is there . . . We must not let evil overcome us, but we must overcome evil," he wrote. That ability to share the grief and reach out to others who are suffering, even when his own people have been suffering for decades, is a mark of his faith and compassion.

When the Free Burma Rangers first formed, "none of them prayed", says Tha-U-Wah-A-Pah. Now, he says, they all pray. "If nothing else happens here, the relationships that have been built between each one of us and between us and God have made it worthwhile," he adds.

But plenty more happens with the Free Burma Rangers. More than any other group of relief workers, they reach the most needy and the most remote places in Burma to bring help, hope and love. They also take the most risks, going right into the centre of the conflict. Since the core group's establishment, they have done over 40 missions into Burma, and trained over 30 teams. Since 1998 they have usually done at least five missions a year, each one a month long. Some of their trips involve hundreds of miles of walking – one trip to Karen State was only about 70 miles deep as the crow flies, but involved 350 miles of walking. They often walk 20 miles or more in a day, stay overnight in a village or in the jungle, carry out a clinic the next day, and walk through the night to get to the next location. On each mission, an average of 2,000 patients are treated and at least 4,000 receive help of some sort.

The work involves medical relief, documentation of human rights violations, and spiritual encouragement. The teams always include medics, videographers, photographers, pastors and musicians. They pull teeth, deliver babies, sew up wounds, treat diseases, perform basic surgical operations and sing songs. The Barking Deer, for example, when she is not treating patients can be found, accompanied by the Mad Dog on a guitar, sitting beside a stream in a clearing in the jungle singing in Karen:

Let us try to find the miracles that the Lord showed us in the past
There are many fields of life laid before you.
. . . They need you and me
To show the world that the Lord is as alive as He has ever been.

The Mad Dog has another song, a memory of his childhood and an aspiration for how life in Kawthoolei could be:

Daw Na Range is the place I was born.
It's green, fresh, a wonderful place.
You and I used to sing by the stream
That flows down the mountain.
I can't forget my childhood days.[4]

But in addition to the missions themselves, providing aid and encouragement to people otherwise bereft of both, training other teams to do the same kind of work is perhaps even more important, because the Free Burma Rangers, however miraculous their story, cannot be everywhere.

"The purpose of the training is to train, equip and inspire you to serve your people and help them get freedom," Tha-U-Wah-A-Pah told a gathering of representatives of different ethnic nationalities from Burma at one training session in Karen territory organised in partnership with the National Democratic Front (NDF).

"We call ourselves the Free Burma Rangers because we want everyone in Burma to be free. A Ranger is one who can go alone, or go in pairs. No matter what the obstacles, he will always try. If a Ranger has a weapon, he can fight. If he has no weapon, he can still do something to help. No one can stop the Free Burma Rangers from serving and loving other people. And no one can stop you from serving your people," said Tha-U-Wah-A-Pah to the trainees.

In explaining the Free Burma Rangers, Tha-U-Wah-A-Pah calls it a "movement" rather than an organisation. "It is a movement to serve the people," he tells the ethnic national-ities. "It is always under the authority of the local people. The Free Burma Rangers have no authority. Our aim is to help you to help the people, and to help you improve your organisa-tions."

Although he works with and serves all people regardless of religion, Tha-U-Wah-A-Pah never hides his faith. "I believe in God," he told a gathering of ethnic leaders. "I never see God but I believe in my heart that God made the world and all the people, and he made each one of us different, but we are all God's children. Some of you are Christian, some Buddhist, some Muslim, some have no religion, some worship spirits. I understand God only a little. I understand God's love. He sent his son Jesus to help us. But I believe God is much bigger than my understanding and so we can work together."

He continued: "Every person is flesh and blood and has a brain. But that's not all. Inside, we have a spirit which can communicate with God. And this spirit, no one can kill."

Later, he explained why he does what he does. "I do not work for the CIA," he emphasised. "I am not a big tiger, I am only a small dog. But the small dog goes into the jungle, and he sees a bad thing. He barks, and he comes back. He tells his master, but his master is very busy. So the dog goes to other places to find other friends, and goes back to help. One small dog cannot fight a tiger. But many dogs can do something."

"In officer training school I did not care about God except on Sundays," Tha-U-Wah-A-Pah admitted to the assembled group. "I would go and pray. If I had a problem I would ask God to help me. But if I had no problem I didn't care and I didn't listen to God. I didn't do what He wanted me to do. I was a very stupid man."

Before every mission, the Free Burma Rangers get together to talk and pray. If there are any misunderstandings or issues that need to be resolved, they resolve them then. They are given the opportunity to confess their sins to one another. Tha-U-Wah-A-Pah shares his thoughts and confesses his sins along with the rest of the team, thereby establishing a sense of trust and fellowship that is exceptional for such a multi-ethnic group. "We forgive each other and we go into the mission clean," he explains.

The Black Monkey emphasises the importance of prayer. "I don't want to rely on myself or man," he said. "We always pray." He described one mission into an area of heavy fighting. Two Karen soldiers had already been captured by the Tatmadaw. "Before going in we prayed with all our strength. We asked God to open the way for us. If He wanted us to go, if He opened the way, we would follow, but if He told us to go back, we would go back," he said. "We had to cross a big road which was very dangerous. We prayed. Then darkness came and at seven o'clock in the evening an old man rode up on horseback. 'Go on, don't waste time, the Burma Army has moved on and is not there anymore,' he told us. God sent his messenger – He used a man on horseback!"

The Free Burma Rangers' missions are highly dangerous and it is a miracle that Tha-U-Wah-A-Pah and his team are still alive today. They have found themselves encircled by Burma Army troops, but through a combination of the power of prayer and good military intelligence, they have been able to get out. On one mission to Karenni State, for example, the team had gone in and was being pursued by the Burma Army.

"We had been through many burned out villages. We had ten Karenni soldiers with us, and that was all. Three battalions of Burmese – over one thousand troops – were coming to get us. The only possible way out was to get to the top of the nearby mountain and hope and pray for safety," Tha-U-Wah-A-Pah recalls.

"We asked God how we should pray and I felt Him say: 'Just use my name'. So we did just that. We used His name against the powers and principalities, the communications and intelligence networks, the Burmese military ability to conduct an operation."

Prayer – using the Lord's name – worked in their favour. "The next morning we heard that one Burmese unit had gone back, another had got lost and the third was unaccounted for."

In the midst of this the group encountered an elderly Karen man dressed in his best red tunic, with a big smile on his face. Tha-U-Wah-A-Pah asked him: "How can you smile? The Burmese soldiers have burned your village!" The man replied: "The Burma Army can kill my body, but not my spirit. They can burn our village and our church, but today is Sunday – the Lord's day – so it is a happy day!"

The Free Burma Rangers started to make their way back to Thailand, and crossed over the Salween River. But they were still not safe. It was 7 p.m. and the team had got out on to the riverbank on the Thai side. They were walking along thinking they had survived. The shore was covered in white sand and dense jungle was just 100 yards away. But suddenly, as if out of nowhere, the Burmese military came by in a boat.

"Run," said the Mad Dog.

They got into a dip and hid. They could see a column of Tatmadaw troops approaching. They prayed. "Lord, stop the Burmese in Jesus name." All the Free Burma Rangers had to defend themselves were knives – no guns. "We would kill them or die trying to defend ourselves, but we really did not want to kill them, or to die," Tha-U-Wah-A-Pah said. As they prayed, however, they saw God's hand of protection at work once again. "The Burmese military boat overshot the place we were hiding in by about 40 yards and was not able to reverse."

That was still not the end of it, however. Six hours later the group was progressing down the Salween and they could hear the Tatmadaw again. Fortunately, because the Burmese soldiers were talking, the Free Burma Rangers were able to slip past and get away.

"We all felt that something was not right. We prayed against the spirit of fear and murder in this land. As we prayed, everything lifted off us."

On another occasion, the Free Burma Rangers were in Dooplaya district in Karen State, the site of a terrible massacre in 2002. In scenes reminiscent of Moses and the Israelites, the Free Burma Rangers led 96 internally displaced Karen people to safety in Thailand. But they were pursued by the Burma Army. "They tried to shell and mortar us. They actually killed two of our guys and wounded another, and captured one," explained Tha-U-Wah-A-Pah. As the group approached the border, they realised that five Burma Army battalions had surrounded them. They decided to do an all-out push to Thailand, walking without stopping for a whole day. "The kids and the old people could barely walk," Tha-U-Wah-A-Pah said. "The kids were sick with malaria, and we were still eight hours' walk from Thailand."

Finally, the group decided to stop, one kilometre from the trail system, and they set up a perimeter defence. They discussed what to do next. If they went south through the mountains, it would take three or four more days. They had no more food. But if they went through the rice fields they would be open targets for Burma Army mortars. They prayed, and then they heard footsteps. Tha-U-Wah-A-Pah describes the scene:

"An old Karen with a bald, funny looking head – like a friendly Gollum – appeared, laughing. He said: 'The Burmese know you're here and think you will not dare to cross the fields but will go around the mountains. So they are waiting for you in the mountains. So, go across the rice fields.'"

The Burma Army had poor intelligence. As Tha-U-Wah-A-Pah later heard on the radio, the Burmese soldiers believed that the group he was leading was not 96 refugees and a few aid workers, protected by a handful of Karen soldiers, but instead a group of 96 heavily armed soldiers, nine Free Burma Rangers, led by a British special forces commander. For this reason the Tatmadaw decided not to attack. The conversation between the Burmese commander and his superiors could be intercepted by the KNLA radios:

"I refuse to attack them," said the commander. "They are heavily armed."

"You idiot," his superior barked back. "They are IDPs not soldiers. Attack."

"No," replied the commander's radio man. "We cannot go now. The commander has malaria and a high fever."

At 2 a.m. the refugees and the Free Burma Rangers rose and had a prayer meeting with lighted candles. They started walking at 3 a.m, and by noon they were safely back in Thailand.

Once, the Black Monkey went on a mission to the IDPs alone, without the protection of soldiers or villagers. While he reached the IDPs safely and was able to distribute aid and bring encouragement to them, the difficulty came when he wanted to leave and return to Thailand. "There were two ways out. The first was to go straight to the border, but that meant going through an area full of Burma Army soldiers. The other way was to go an indirect route – through an area with many landmines," he said. He prayed, and chose the second route. "At least with the landmine area, I could be hurt or killed, but not captured." He got directions, but then got lost. However, after more prayer he found his way and reached the border – unharmed. "I praised God and asked him to lead me always."

Tha-U-Wah-A-Pah's wife is a key player in his ministry, and is willing to put her faith in God. But when her husband is gone on long missions deep inside Burma, and is out of communication, life is not easy. On one occasion, she received a report that the Burma Army had captured a foreigner. Knowing that her husband was at the top of the junta's hit list, she went through hours of anguish, not knowing what might happen. She could only imagine what they might do to him. She knew that if they caught him, the chances of her seeing him again were slim. However, a day or two later, word came out that he was safe and that it was another foreigner who had been caught. That foreigner was later released.

On some missions, she accompanies the Free Burma Rangers, carrying her two young daughters with her. Before the children were born, she did some of the deeper missions – now they go on short trips close to the Thai border, but leave the longer missions to Tha-U-Wah-A-Pah.

One year, they went to Pa'an district, a most remote part of Kawthoolei where the people had never seen a white person. It had been an area of heavy fighting, but they decided to keep going. "If God sends you somewhere, or gives you something to do, you should do it until He moves you," she believes. She recalls a picture she received while praying in a time of some danger. "I was in the middle of a lake and the water became too deep. I started treading water but I was scared. I decided to swim for the bank and have a rest. But when I got to the bank, I saw Jesus still out in the middle of the lake. He was holding his arms out and saying 'I am here with you'. I decided it was better to be with Jesus in the middle of the lake than to be on my own on the bank."

Such faith has its rewards. She recalls a village headman who came to Tha-U-Wah-A-Pah and asked for prayer. He was in his sixties, a member of a sect which believed in the Old Testament God without Jesus, and he had been addicted to heroin for years. Tha-U-Wah-A-Pah and Htoo Htoo Lay prayed for him. The next year they saw him, beaming with joy. He had not taken heroin since the day they had prayed for him.

Tha-U-Wah-A-Pah's wife says the difference in spirit between the Christian villages and the other villages is palpable. "In the non-Christian villages, there are usually no schools, no clinics, and a lot of fear. In a Christian village you can see how faith triumphs over fear – people are not afraid of the spirits which they used to fear, in the rocks and plants. Even if people are illiterate, they have a sense of God's care for them, a sense of pride and motivation. In non-Christian villages, kids do not seem to play as much – they are afraid."

In addition to the dangerous missions deep inside Burma, Tha-U-Wah-A-Pah and his wife have been active in communicating the needs of Burma to the outside world and providing practical ways for people in other countries to help. His wife, for example, initiated a scheme called the "Good Life Club".

"The inspiration came from John 10:10 where Jesus says 'The thief comes only to steal and kill and destroy; I have come that they may have life, and have it to the full'," says Tha-U-Wah-A-Pah's wife.

The Good Life Club provides "tangible ways in which kids in the United States and elsewhere can help," she explains. Children in the United States and other countries are encouraged to gather plastic zip-lock bags and fill them with useful gifts – basic medicine, toothpaste, hats, nail-clippers, vitamins, toys – and add a postcard with a picture and some Bible verses of encouragement. "It is intended to contain things that will help kids in the jungle in Burma live a day longer," she says. "It is based on the model of the Samaritan's Purse, but it has to be small. The internally displaced people are on the run so they have to be able to carry it."

Tha-U-Wah-A-Pah is not always the only foreigner on Free Burma Ranger missions. Sometimes he is accompanied by others, such as Louisiana dentist Shannon Allison, a former special forces soldier. He voluntarily uses his holidays to go on trips with the Free Burma Rangers right into the heart of the conflict zone. Allison is honest about the fact that he enjoys the excitement – but he is also attached to the deeper issues. "Absolutely it's an adventure," he admits. "But there's a cause here which far outweighs anything else."[5]

Burma is a battle between good and evil, in Allison's view. "It is the only place I have ever seen that is going backwards," he says.[6] There was once a beautiful, thriving culture and now the Karen and other ethnic nationalities, in his depiction, are reduced to living out of streams and fires on the road. "That's the death knell of a race."

He believes what is happening is genocide. "When it destroys the character of a race, it is genocide. And as long as the world doesn't care, they are going to continue to do what they want to do."

Doh Say agrees. "What the Burmese are using here is worse than ethnic cleansing. We strongly believe they are practising genocide here. The Burmese regime is systematically destroying all the villages. In the past they killed people with a gun or a knife, but now, after 1996 and 1997, across the country they carry out forced relocation programmes. And they can say to the world: 'No we are not killing the people any more.' "

Allison's involvement, then, is about "literally fighting evil", something he sees as a responsibility. "You don't ask for it, but there is some point in time that good has to stand up against evil, and even against overwhelming odds there are times when you have just got to do it. You don't turn away and run, you have got to make a stand."

If the Karen and other armed resistance gave up their arms now, Allison adds, "they are slowly going to get squashed". Then the Karen tribe will no longer exist. "When you see that happening in front of your eyes in the modern day it is scary," he says. "It is the same thing the Nazis did to the Jews."[7]

Allison's trips with the Free Burma Rangers have entailed more than their fair share of danger, but also of miraculous escapes. At the end of one trip, Tha-U-Wah-A-Pah and Allison emerged from the jungle across the border into Thailand, straight into the arms of a Thai soldier. The Thais do not take kindly to illegal border crossings, and the soldier was startled to see two foreigners who were clearly not just average hikers. They had been inside the jungle for a month, and they probably looked like that was the case.

"Where have you been?" asked the Thai soldier, knowing full well what the answer was.

Tha-U-Wah-A-Pah believes the best policy in these circumstances is honesty. They are not doing anything morally wrong – smuggling drugs or trading arms – and in fact are doing a lot of good, so they should have nothing to hide. Honesty also has the advantage that is disarms the questioner, who expects a convoluted excuse.

"Oh, we've just been in Burma," replied Tha-U-Wah-A-Pah, in his best Thai.

The soldier blinked with surprise. "And what were you doing there?"

"We were trying to help the people, delivering medicines to the displaced people, treating the sick, giving out Bibles, praying with people, helping them," explained Tha-U-Wah-A-Pah.

Then, before the disoriented Thai soldier could ask another question, Tha-U-Wah-A-Pah added:

"Let me introduce my friend Shannon, he's a dentist from

America. He's the best dentist in the world. Do you have any teeth problems?"

The soldier nodded. "Yes, as a matter of fact I have a real pain in the back here," he said, opening his jaw and pointing at a cavity.

Allison opened his toolbox and asked the soldier to open wide his mouth. "Let's see – yes, you need a filling here, and one there, and some cleaning here. I'll do it now." With that he took out his best equipment and set to work. When he finished, the soldier was delighted – and waved them through without another word.

But the lighter-hearted moments should not obscure the harsh realities of what the Free Burma Rangers witness. On one trip, they met a Karen man whose two children had been burned alive by the Burma Army. As he told the team what had happened, he wept. "I don't understand why they killed my children. They didn't even know their right from their left hand."

In June 2002, the Free Burma Rangers brought out pictures, taken by a Karen relief team earlier, of a massacre in Htee Law Bleh, Dooplaya district, Karen State which shocked the international community. On 28th April, 2002 twelve people were killed by the Burma Army's Infantry Battalion 78. Overall in central Dooplaya district, from April to June 2002, over 5,000 people were displaced, six villages burned, five churches torched, fifteen villagers murdered including children as young as two years old, and over 1,000 people were in hiding in the jungle trying to escape to Thailand. Three pastors, Happy Htoo, See Pa Thru and Pareh, were captured and tortured for five days outside their churches.

"This is a brutal reign of terror," the Free Burma Rangers' report concluded. "The feeling of fear and hopelessness was palpable . . . The sight of babies crying and children in rags fleeing the attacks of the Burma Army is horrible and wrong.

Families with all their belongings on their backs have to struggle through dense jungle as they cannot use proper trails because of Burma Army ambushes. They are hunted, shelled and driven like animals."

In one of the attacks, Burma Army Column Commander Khin Mau Kyi, leading Infantry Battalion 78 as it carried out these atrocities, summed up the attitude of the regime as he urinated on the head of a Buddhist monk. "I do not respect any religion," he said. "My religion is the trigger of my gun."

A six-year-old boy was shot during the massacre at Htee Law Bleh, but miraculously he played dead and the soldiers left him alone. Although his grandmother was killed, he survived and was later treated by the Free Burma Rangers team.

Later that year, Light Infantry Battalion 235 attacked the villagers of Ler Mu Plaw, with heavy weapons and small arms. Six people were killed. An eight-year-old girl, Naw Moo Day Wah, was among the victims. She was shot in the stomach by the Tatmadaw, and was in a coma. Karen medics arrived on the scene six days later and found that she needed hospitalisation but there was no hospital or clinic nearby. The girl was reported dead ten days after she had been shot. "I felt angry that any soldier could shoot a child like that, and her sweet face haunted me," Tha-U-Wah-A-Pah said. "I remember thinking 'this is evil and so wrong – this is what we go in for, this is what we risk all for'."

Four months later, Tha-U-Wah-A-Pah returned to the village, at least ten days' walk from the border. To his amazement he saw the girl who he thought had died. In his report called *The Flight of the Jungle Chicken*, he wrote: "I dropped to one knee and, holding her hand, prayed a prayer of thanks to our good Father," he recalled. "She had recovered and was well. The bullet was still inside her but it gave her no problems. I am grateful to God for every miracle even in the face of other great losses."

In June 2003, the Free Burma Rangers visited Pa-an district, and interviewed victims of Burma Army attacks. One man, captured and forced to be a porter for the Burma Army, described witnessing the torture of a 30-year-old man who had been tied up by his wrists and suspended in the air from the ceiling of a bamboo hut. Underneath him, the soldiers lit a fire and started to burn him alive. Although the soldiers eventually let him down because other villagers pleaded with them, it was too late. The man died of severe burns that night.

Another man, a village leader, told the team he had been tied up by his neck by soldiers, including a company commander, Tun Win. His hands were tied behind his back and his ankles were tied. He was kept in that position for two weeks. Throughout that time, soldiers beat him with their rifle butts on his head, knocked his teeth out, kicked him and beat him all over his body with their guns. "He felt like he lost his mind many times," the Free Burma Rangers report. "Three times, the Burma Army soldiers asked other porters to dig a hole to bury him in after they killed him, but he was never killed. He asked the Burma Army to kill him because he was suffering so much. After fourteen days they brought him back to his village, but told him he had to go and meet the Burma Army soldiers every day. He did that for two days and then fled."

A former DKBA soldier who had defected told the Free Burma Rangers how remorseful he felt about the terrible things he had done. He had participated in the burning of Si Pa Lay village, south of Htee Hta Blu Hta, on 18th October, 2002. "The DKBA does not care for the people," he admitted. "It only takes what it wants and causes the people to suffer. I don't want to be a DKBA soldier any more. I ran away to join the KNU, to help my people to be free. The Burma Army will not help us. It uses the DKBA."

The Free Burma Rangers do not fit with the stereotypical image of a missionary group. Although they do not seek combat, they do carry guns – something many in comfortable Western churches find difficult to come to terms with. But they are not mercenaries. They are armed, and they work with the armed resistance groups, because that is the nature of the place where God has called them to work. If they were not armed, they would be killed, and the humanitarian relief they take in would be captured and taken for Burma Army supplies. And there is little purpose in that.

But although they are unconventional, they are absolutely grounded in biblical teaching, following Jesus' command to love our neighbour and to trust God. One of their guiding Scriptures is Zechariah 4:6, which says: " 'Not by might nor by power, but by my Spirit,' says the Lord."

Love is at the centre of their mission. "The teams believe that the dictators of Burma cannot stop people from loving and serving each other," says Tha-U-Wah-A-Pah. "They shine a light where there is darkness."

In June 2003, soon after Daw Aung San Suu Kyi was arrested again, a Free Burma Ranger team leader wrote this message, which was circulated internationally. It sums up the urgency of the situation and the courage of the Free Burma Rangers in trying to help:

As we were treating IDPs in Karen state at a recently burned village, deeper inside Burma Aung San Suu Kyi had just been arrested and many of her supporters murdered. Ethnic or Burman, no one is safe from the terror of the dictators of Burma. We have helped to treat and pray for women who have been raped by soldiers of the Burma Army, children who were shot, parents who saw their children thrown into a fire and many others who have endured evil. They screamed for help but no one came to save them. The world knows these things are happening. In this world, actions fall into two categories: acceptable and unacceptable. Raping little girls, murder and burning villages is unacceptable. If these things are truly unacceptable what must we do as individuals and nations? Now is the time that all people must choose where they stand, with the people of Burma or with the dictators. In the face of evil we will not flee. We will act with love, with prayer and with our lives. God bless you.

NOTES

1 Don Richardson, *Eternity in their Hearts*
2 Ibid.
3 BBC, *The Forgotten War*
4 Ibid.
5 Ibid.
6 Ibid.
7 Ibid.

CHAPTER EIGHT

THE YOUNG WHITE BROTHERS

The Lord's chosen children,
People expecting God,
Blessed you are.
You've been persecuted
And enslaved as well.
The white brother liberators
God sent them back.
A Karen anthem[1]

The Karen legend that a young white brother would come across the ocean to bring them the lost book and to help them has proven to be true. Not only did Adoniram Judson come carrying the Bible, but he has been followed by many others. Major Seagrim and Tha-U-Wah-A-Pah followed in Judson's footsteps. So too have men like James Mawdsley, Saw Serky, Dr Martin Panter and politicians such as Baroness Cox, Lord Alton and Congressman Joseph Pitts. They have all helped in different ways, making sacrifices of various types, to help the Karen in their time of need.

Dr Martin Panter, for example, has been working with the Karen since 1989. A British-born general practitioner living in Australia, from his childhood Dr Panter wanted to be a medical missionary. At the age of five or six, he read Paul White's books about life as a "jungle doctor" in Tanzania. A whole series of books came onto the market – *Jungle Doctor Operates, Jungle Doctor on Safari, Jungle Doctor in Trouble* – and the young boy devoured them all. That was what he wanted to be when he grew up, he thought.

Some years after qualifying in medicine and getting married, Dr Panter and his wife did a Youth With A Mission (YWAM) Discipleship Training Scheme (DTS). It changed their life. Memories of the *Jungle Doctor* came alive in Dr Panter's mind and rekindled the desire for outreach to those most cut off from outside assistance. But he was conscious that he had little background in tropical medicine, and decided to rectify that. He took a Diploma at the Liverpool School of Tropical Medicine in 1988, where he studied in detail the causes and treatment of malaria, dengue fever and "African sleeping sickness". He also learned the value of preventative medicine. "I realised intuitively that sitting behind a desk with a stethoscope around my neck handing out pills from little bottles would achieve little or nothing in the long term," he says.

Instead, he learned that "the provision of clean water supply, the sanitary disposal of waste products, the education of women – at least to literate or semi-literate levels – and a basic understanding of nutritional needs were the most important preliminary necessities in the provision of health care. It was a sobering but also liberating discovery." He also spent three weeks studying toilet systems – "pit latrines, ventilated pit latrines, improved ventilated pit latrines" – which, working in the jungle with the Karen, he found to be information "of inestimable value".

And so in 1989 he found himself on a two-hour journey in a boat going down the Salween River, in flood at the time, to Manerplaw. He recalled the scene:

"We got to Mae Hong Son, and there was just an enormous mass of muddy water. But due to the great skill of the Karen boatman, we were able to navigate around the carcasses of dead animals in the water, passing beautiful teak plantations and herds of elephants drinking at the riverside."

When the boat reached the junction of the mighty Salween River and the much smaller Moei, Dr Panter experienced for the first time the effects of such a confluence. "With the river in flood, it appeared quite terrifying," he said. He was met by "a swirling angry seething mass of turbulent brown water, approximately two to three kilometres across".

Upon reaching Manerplaw, the KNU headquarters, Dr Panter met with General Bo Mya. Eager to get to work immediately organising programmes for medical training, conducting surveys of the health care needs of villages, establishing systems for preventative medicine, Dr Panter was to be disappointed. "The first shock on arriving in Manerplaw was to discover that the Karen were not about to be pushed or coerced into my Western programmes of disease control or health care advice, however radical, sensible and life changing they were to be," he recalls. The Karen wanted first to get to know him and his family. "It was a painful, though essential, lesson to learn that in Asia especially, and I suspect in many other parts of the world as well, things are accomplished best through the medium of relationship."

So he met with Bo Mya, and it turned out to be simply a chat. "He was cracking Betel nuts with a nut cracker and then chewing the pieces, interspersed with rambutans. He was surrounded by food and fruit, and he offered me a rambutan," recalls Dr Panter. "He asked about my journey, my family, but strangely, he did not ask anything about why I had come."

After a few days, however, Dr Panter was allowed to get to work. He met with the then Karen Health Minister Dr Julius Khoo Thaw, a trained surgeon, who asked the English doctor if he would see a patient suffering from falciparum malaria, jaundice and severe diarrhoea. Then came the invitation

Dr Panter was seeking. He was asked to go into the Karen villages.

Since 1989 Dr Panter has visited the Karen at least twice a year. Until the fall of Manerplaw in 1995, he – and sometimes his wife and three young children – always stayed with General Hla Htoo and his wife in a beautiful teak house on the banks of the Moei, but went deep into the jungle to treat patients and conduct basic medical training for Karen villagers. One of his earliest trips into Kawthoolei involved a twelve-hour hike up and down mountains, covering about 20 kilometres and reaching a village after dusk.

Dr Panter treated a variety of diseases and injuries in his trips to the jungles of Kawthoolei, some more undesirable than others. In one village he was asked to conduct a clinic, despite having very few instruments or drugs with him. A long line of villagers were waiting patiently. One patient was a lady who claimed to be 100 years old. She had only one tooth, but it was badly decayed and painful. She wanted it extracted. Dr Panter, not by training a dentist but instead a doctor with an adventurous spirit who had done a two-hour dental course and had some dental equipment, gave the tooth a pull and it slipped out easily.

On another trip to the Karen, Dr Panter went to Htee Hta and as he arrived in the village, a young Karen soldier called Sonny hobbled over and asked the doctor for help. When Dr Panter inquired what the problem was, the soldier lowered his *longyi* to reveal a large hole in his right buttock. "It was both wide and deep enough to admit an entire clenched fist, as far as the wrist," Dr Panter explained. The soldier had been shot at while travelling down the river nine months previously, and the shell had gone in through his right thigh. "How it had missed vital structures such as the main sciatic nerve to the leg, or the main blood vessels supplying it, must have been close to miraculous," said Dr Panter.

The doctor asked the soldier to come to the village hospital the next day. Fortunately the wound was fairly clean, but it was deeper than it had first looked, and extended almost to the rear side of the hip joint. Dr Panter was not convinced he could do much to help but offered to try. There was only local anaesthetic available, so Dr Panter gave Sonny a large piece of wood to bite on as he cleaned the wound and sewed him up.

Such good deeds sometimes have undesired rewards. Sonny's family were delighted that their son's wound had finally been treated, and wanted to thank the doctor for his work. In honour of the doctor, therefore, they announced that they would shoot and cook a monkey.

Dr Panter wasted no time in assuring them that he was not expecting a special meal as he had been happy to help. His hosts would not listen. He then reminded them that he had to leave early in the morning and that it was already late. It was not surely a breakfast dish?

But there was no escape. The family told the doctor that monkey was in fact the ideal dish with which to begin the day, and it would nourish and sustain the group on their long journey back to Thailand. There was nothing more the doctor could do except graciously accept the hospitality. He recalls the scene:

There was a huge iron cooking pot over a charcoal fire steaming away merrily. The lid was lifted with evident pride by the chief chef, who was in this case the patient's older sister. There staring up at me were the lifeless eyes of the hapless victim. I winced involuntarily, not only from being totally unaccustomed to viewing a whole dead mammal being cooked, but even more so a whole primate.

But this was not the end of it. There was a particular part of the body of the monkey that is always reserved for special guests. Dr Panter fell into the category of special guest, and so he was presented with a dish of the monkey's bowels, along with its contents, known as "monkey doodoo". He was assured that since monkeys live off leaves and flowers, the bowels are safe and, indeed, nutritious.

When Dr Panter actually took a few mouthfuls of the monkey doodoo, he found it was not actually as bad, in terms of taste, as the concept suggested. "It was surprisingly mild. It was more like cheese than anything else," he said. His hosts inquired how it was and, being polite, he tried to summon up some enthusiasm. Delighted, the family promised as he left that on his next trip he should let them know in good time that he was coming. "We will go out and hunt many monkeys," they pledged. He made a mental note to return to Htee Htar completely unannounced in future.

Two years later, Dr Panter arrived at Manerplaw to be greeted at the riverside by Sonny, dressed in uniform and with a sub-machine gun slung from his shoulder. He pulled down his *longyi* to reveal a clean, slightly indented scar on his left buttock. "I said a silent prayer of thanks as the result was far better than I hoped or certainly deserved," said Dr Panter.

Several years after he first went to the Karen, Dr Panter identified the need for eye specialists to treat landmine blast injuries. In many cases the eyes could not be saved, but in some corrective surgery was possible. Another need was for cataract operations among the elderly. Dr Panter advertised in the Christian Medical Journal, and two eye specialists volunteered. They now go at least twice a year and carry out cataract operations among the Karen and Karenni. He recalls the result of one particular cataract operation:

"The incredible joy to be seen on the face of an elderly patient, totally blind for some years and restored to the land of sight by a relatively simple operation, makes any deprivations, difficulties or dangers fade into insignificance in contrast."

But Dr Panter, and the eye doctors, knew that more important than treatment was training. "As with all our other activities the aim here is to train up some of the Karen to be their own local opthalmologists in future years," he says.

Another important element of Dr Panter's work was teaching the Karen preventative measures. On one of his early trips to Manerplaw he noted the large number of cases of cerebral malaria, a disease which can develop so fast that you can be well at breakfast, have a fever at lunch and be dead by dinner time. On the next visit, therefore, he brought with him over four kilometres' worth of mosquito netting. He and his team showed the Karen how to make mosquito nets, and they left feeling that they had really made progress. Now at least some of the Karen will have some protection against malaria. However, he came back later that year, and found that the netting was strung up alongside the river – the Karen had turned them into fishing nets.

Not willing to give up, Dr Panter and his family, and the two eye doctors, decided to put together a series of drama sketches for the Karen, to illustrate the importance of mosquito nets. So one of them played the part of a healthy person, and another was the mosquito. They demonstrated that when the net was up, the mosquito could not get in, and the person stayed healthy – but when there was no net, or holes in the net, the mosquito gets in, bites and then the person falls sick. The dramas had some effect and in following years the number of mosquito nets in use increased.

The Christian faith of many of the Karen and their "most extraordinary generosity and sacrifice" inspired Dr Panter, as it did Major Seagrim and the soldiers in the Second World War. "When they have almost nothing, they give us whatever they have," he observes. "If a Burmese unit was in front of us, the Karen would put themselves between us and the Burmese soldiers. And even under extraordinary persecution and hardship, they retain a dignity and a peace in their lives which is unworldly." For example, when Dr Panter was in Wang Ka when it was shelled, he noted that while "there was heavy artillery and shells pouring down," there was "no sense of panic or disorder among the Karen. They prayed. One of the leaders put up Psalms all around the walls of a hut, surrounding the soldiers."

However, that generosity and openness had also, in Dr Panter's view, caused a naivety and innocence which is open to abuse. As a Christian he is concerned about the development of "some quite wacky" sects such as the Garner Ted Armstrong and Herbert W Armstrong movement, and also the behaviour of some missionaries who are "over the top". Some foreign missionaries, he claims, have come in with totally false prophesies. "General Bo Mya once said to me that if the Karen people had believed all the prophesies they had heard they would have been free 50 years ago. But it hasn't stopped them trusting God."

Dr Panter also disapproves of some medical practices deployed by other foreign volunteers. "One completely way-out doctor came with a team and was just handing out drugs willy-nilly," he says. "My philosophy is that medics should come to support the local doctors, who are very capable, rather than coming in to do it themselves."

The Karens' innocence, however, is accompanied by an Old Testament intolerance of immorality. Dr Panter tells of visiting the prison in Htee Htar where some of the inmates had been jailed for adultery, a crime which carried a ten-year sentence. Alcohol was banned and soldiers caught drinking were punished severely. "It's like a time-warp," he says.

Dr Panter started out working with the Karen on a purely medical, humanitarian basis, though it was fuelled by his Christian faith. However, what he saw of the suffering in Kawthoolei turned Dr Panter from jungle doctor to passionate advocate, and he became a champion for human rights. He has been prepared to risk his own life and his family's at times. On one mission, staying at Manerplaw, the Karen intelligence told him that the Burmese were planning a major offensive, involving air strikes followed by infantry attacks, for the following day. There were two battalions poised to move into the area he was intending to visit, on the very day they were to arrive.

He faced an agonising decision, because he had his children – a thirteen-year-old daughter, Rachel, a nine-year-old daughter Juliet, and a three-year-old son, Nathaniel – with him. "I knew from experience what the Burmese soldiers do. Not only do they rape and kill, but they torture. They use children to walk in front of the soldiers as human minesweepers. So I knew what would happen if we were captured," he says. But reassurance came from Psalm 27:

The Lord is my light and my salvation – whom shall I fear?
The Lord is the stronghold of my life – of whom shall I be afraid?
When evil men advance against me to devour my flesh,
When my enemies and my foes attack me,
They will stumble and fall.
Though an army besiege me,
My heart will not fear;
Though war break out against me,
Even then will I be confident.

He decided, with the eye specialists, to go ahead with the visit to the village that was reportedly a target for attack. They were walking right into the enemy's lair armed with nothing except faith in the Lord as their stronghold and salvation. But that was all they needed. The Burma Army attack never occurred. Apparently an air strike was scheduled to take place as soon as the morning mists cleared. But for the first time in living memory, instead of clearing, huge clouds billowed up causing a deep and completely impenetrable wall of mist. Burmese planes could be heard overhead but their fuel ran so low they had to ditch the bombs, almost all of which fell on their own troops underneath, apart from one which killed two Karen chickens.[2]

Dr Panter believes in the value of solidarity, of coming and just being with the Karen for a time, reminding them that they are not forgotten. The importance of this was underlined to him on one visit to Mae La refugee camp. When the group was leaving, Pastor Simon's wife turned to Dr Panter's daughter Juliet. "When are you coming again? We live for your visits," she said. "The fact that we identify with them, but haven't offered them the earth, means a lot," said Dr Panter. "We have tried to weep with them. And their generosity to us is not pretentious – it is a genuine response from their hearts."

One of Dr Panter's significant contributions to the Karen struggle has been to introduce Baroness Caroline Cox to the situation. A courageous human rights campaigner and a Deputy Speaker of the House of Lords, Baroness Cox is someone any resistance force would do well to have on side. Her commitment, passion and sacrifice, as well as her influence and articulate presentation of the facts make her an outstanding ambassador for the oppressed and persecuted. In 1992 Dr Panter came into contact with her organisation, Christian Solidarity Worldwide, and did not miss the opportunity to engage her interest in the cause closest to his heart. She was already dedicated to Sudan, Nagorno Karabakh, Russia and Poland – there is never a shortage of concerns on her agenda – but she listened and accepted an invitation to visit the Karen.

Baroness Cox has visited the Thai–Burmese border areas at least once a year since then, and initiated many debates in the British House of Lords to be a voice for the voiceless people of Burma. "Her speeches in the House of Lords and robust defence of their rights has had a powerful effect on promoting spirit and hope among the Karen and Karenni, who have been greatly helped by Caroline's unceasing efforts to be an advocate and a voice for them," Dr Panter says. "What impressed me most of all was the graciousness, kindness and respect she had for the simplest, the poorest and the most wretched of the refugees. She spoke to them with love and compassion."[3]

But she did not simply visit refugees and show compassion. Just as she flies into the face of danger in Sudan and Indonesia, Baroness Cox showed little hesitation about crossing the border illegally to visit the Karen resistance. She stayed in Manerplaw, but sometimes went deeper into the jungle. On one visit, she wanted to go and see the front line Karen soldiers, to encourage them and to see first-hand the situation. The Karen offered to take her to the top of a mountain peak, where there was a KNLA outpost directly facing the Burma Army on Sleeping Dog Mountain. It involved an extremely arduous hike up a steep mountain, with the climate very hot and humid, and even Baroness Cox found it hard going. But she was not phased by the fact that the area was heavily mined and the Burmese soldiers were just a few kilometres away, though as she struggled up the mountain, she did think to herself "Caroline Cox, you are a grandmother with six grandchildren. It's time you grew up and stopped doing these crazy trips!"[4]

In the midst of such thoughts, her attention was captured by the sound of bell ringing in the middle of the jungle. A keen campanologist herself, she was intrigued as to where this sound came from. They followed the sound and discovered a little Karen church. The bell was made from a sawn-off top of a Burmese bomb. "Instead of swords into ploughshares, it was bombs into bells," she says.[5]

The group came to a ridge, and had to walk along the crest of the ridge in full view of Burmese snipers just 300 metres away. It was the only way to reach the KNLA outpost. But Baroness Cox, and Dr Panter who was with her, knew the dangers and still felt it was important to visit the soldiers. If anything, they perhaps underestimated the value of their visit. They were the first ever foreigners to visit these particular troops on this mountain outpost, and as they reached the top the Karen soldiers stood amazed to see them. "We thought we had been forgotten, that nobody knew about our battle," they told Baroness Cox. The idea that a Deputy Speaker of the British House of Lords would risk her life to visit them impressed them deeply. As they talked, they had to keep their heads down below the ridge, and try to carry on a conversation interspersed with ground fire from below. "It meant a lot to them to know they weren't forgotten, that people cared enough to come and visit them," she explained. The soldiers told her that her visit gave them the strength to carry on their struggle.

Encouraging the soldiers and refugees is an important part of Baroness Cox's missions, but it is not the only purpose. Fully aware of her own opportunities for influence in Parliament and in political and diplomatic circles, she makes a point of taking detailed testimonies of human rights violations and bringing the evidence out to present to the international community, with the credibility that comes with her position and the authenticity that comes through having been to the front lines. So when, for example, she and Dr Panter were presented with claims that the Burmese had been using biological and chemical warfare on the ethnic minorities, she took the evidence back to Britain to be tested.

Karen witnesses told Baroness Cox that they had seen weather balloons[6] and devices dropped into their territory,[7] and that shortly afterwards there was a severe outbreak of cholera and virulent kinds of gastro-intestinal diseases never before experienced in Kawthoolei. People also suffered severe flesh blistering, a sign of mustard gas. One man reported a pungent smell that he had never experienced before soon after a bomb blast, and he suffered third-degree burns from traces of a substance stuck to his skin. Other people fell unconscious and many felt weak and unbalanced for days. According to Dr Panter, "Children play with the balloons, the cholera gets on them, they spread it round the village, and a few days later the Burmese forces come in and most of the people are disabled or dead."

The Karen claimed to have intercepted Burmese military radio messages referring to chemical weapons, instructing all forces to disguise any record of their use, including burning all the weapons cases.

One of the devices, a polystyrene box 18 inches by 8 inches, with a depth of three to four inches, was brought out to show the Baroness. The name of the maker and the identity strip had been removed.

"Interesting," said Baroness Cox. "One for the scientists back home."[8]

She persuaded Dr Panter to take the device back to Britain in his hand luggage, and remarkably it was not detected at either Bangkok or London Heathrow airports. However, when Dr Panter arrived at the House of Lords a few days later to give it back to the Baroness, the security system picked it up. "When I said it was for Baroness Cox, the security officer gave me a wink and signalled me through!" said Dr Panter.

It is Baroness Cox's position in the House of Lords which has been most valuable for the Karen – and for other ethnic groups in Burma. In addition to speaking up on behalf of the Karen, she has been a passionate advocate for the Karenni people, and that was as a result of a copy of *Hansard*, the record of parliamentary debates, finding its way to the Thai–Burmese border!

It was Plyar Reh, the then President of the Karenni National Progressive Party and a devout Catholic, who read one of

Baroness Cox's speeches about the Karen in Hansard, and wrote to her to appeal for help for his people too. So on her next trip to the region, she met with Plyar Reh, Prime Minister General Aung Than Lei and Karenni Foreign Minister Abel Tweed, and heard testimonies which shocked her. In Karenni, she was told, there were at least 80,000 displaced people and only 1,700 Karenni resistance fighters facing over 30 Burma Army battalions.

She heard of one Christian family in the jungle with a tale of the utmost horror. Bau La Gu had been a 55-year-old widow, with four children aged between 10 and 22. The family had been caught on the run by the Burma Army, and their hands were tied behind their backs. One by one, the children – and then their mother – were thrown into the village paddy pounder, a foot-operated machine to grind rice with a wooden pestle weighing 50 kilos. The eldest daughter, aged 22, was forced to watch as her siblings and her mother were pulverised to death. Then she fled.[9]

Baroness Cox was told further horrific stories. Children in Karenni had been hanged from branches and used as target practice by the soldiers. A ten-year-old boy and his eleven-year-old sister had been tied up and thrown into a fire.

All this was going on at the same time as the British Government were holding a trade fair in Rangoon. In 1994 a "British Week" was organised, and another was planned for the following year. On 4th December, 1994, the Ambassador in Rangoon wrote a letter to British companies inviting them to attend:

"In the last twelve months there has been a significant increase in business activity in Myanmar (Burma). I believe that there are now good opportunities opening up here for British business," he wrote. "Within the limitations imposed by our political attitude towards the present government, which remain unchanged, we in the Embassy have been trying to encourage this interest and to see how we might recapture our position as one of Myanmar's traditional trading partners. We initiated this by staging a very successful British Week in March this year."

The Ambassador went on to describe the plans for 1995 – a British trade delegation to coincide with the Myanmar Trade Fair, with "no attendance fee" for British companies but perhaps "a voluntary contribution to our costs". The British Week, attended by 50 companies, was not only a week of business – it included jazz evenings with the British Moire Music Orchestra and cabaret evenings at the Strand Hotel. Baroness Cox was, rightly, furious. She took it up with the Foreign and Commonwealth Office, who, in a letter to her on 18th January, 1996, dismissed such trade events as "a small-scale affair" designed "to correct the distorted image of Britain in Burma". It was not only about trade, the Foreign Office added. "The programme contained important cultural and informational elements." But Baroness Cox would not tolerate such appeasement. In a letter to *The Times* on 29th November, 1995, she noted that "the inappropriateness of such an initiative can hardly be overstated". Due to her protests, and the appeals of others, such trade fairs stopped in February 1996.

But what impressed Baroness Cox about the situation for the Karen and Karenni most was the incredible grace of the people who were suffering. Meredith Nunu, for example, had seen her husband shot dead in front of her and her house burned down. But when asked if she was bitter, she replied: "Of course I miss him, but I have to forgive, just as the Lord's prayer says forgive us our sins as we forgive those who sin against us."[10] Ma Su was another example. Soon after the Burma Army had shelled the refugee camp in Thailand where she and many others were sheltering, Baroness Cox visited. "Everything was burned and destroyed," Baroness Cox

recalled. "Her hut was burned and she had been shot by a
Burmese soldier. I asked how she felt about the soldier who
shot her, and her response: 'I love him. It says in the Bible we
should love our enemies, so of course I love him. He is my
brother.'"

Baroness Cox has introduced and spoken in numerous
debates on Burma in the House of Lords since her involvement
with the Karen and Karenni began and always her speeches
are fuelled with the passion that comes from seeing the situation first-hand. In one debate in December 2002, she charged
the Burmese junta with genocide. The regime, she argued,
"continues to perpetrate gross violations of human rights,
such as the use of forced labour, human minesweepers, child
soldiers, military offensives against innocent civilians, rape,
torture and massacre. Such atrocities in Karen, Karenni, Shan,
Mon, Chin and Arakan states continue unabated. The violations are so systematic, ruthless and comprehensive that they
can justifiably be designated as ethnic cleansing or genocide."[11]

A key ally of Baroness Cox on this issue is Lord Alton of
Liverpool, a committed Catholic and an energetic campaigner
for justice. He founded the Jubilee Campaign, has visited the
Karen several times, and argues vigorously that the actions of
the SPDC in the Karen areas count as "genocide". In a debate
in June 2003, he told the House of Lords that he had taken
over 100 pages of carefully documented examples of human
rights violations in the previous year alone. "I can think of no
other country where so many displaced people are being subjected to a shoot-on-sight policy, yet Her Majesty's Government and the international community continue to pay
relatively little attention to the desperate plight of the Karen,
Karenni and Shan," he argued. He concluded his speech by
posing a question to the British Government: "If this is not
genocide, what is?"[12]

Across the Atlantic, US Congressman Joseph Pitts has championed the cause, and he visited the Karen with Lord Alton early in 2003. In an orphanage in Mae La refugee camp, Karen children, most of whose parents had been killed by the Burma Army, gathered to tell the two men their stories. One little girl began to talk about her father who had died, and as she spoke, tears flowed down her cheeks. Unable to continue, she clapped her hand over her mouth and stopped. A Christian relief worker who was accompanying the group described what happened next. "As the storytelling ended and a sudden moment of awkwardness filled the crowded, dark room, Congressman Pitts sensed the girl's inward pain. He reached out to her and bent down to give her one of his cards . . . He asked the girl if she would please, at a later time, write a letter to him, telling him of her loss, her struggle. He let her know that he cares, that we all do, and that she is loved and will be prayed for. I could see into the future for a moment. I could visualise this young girl's letter arriving on Congressman Pitts' desk in Washington DC months, maybe even a year later. A letter with a prayer. A silent prayer ready to be heard."[13]

Congressman Pitts returned to Washington DC deeply affected by what he had seen and vowing to strengthen his voice and influence for the cause. He did just that by introducing in the US House of Representatives a resolution calling for immediate intervention in Burma. Mr Pitts' resolution points out to the world that the junta is engaged in "ethnic cleansing" which amounts to "genocide under international law". It calls for a number of measures, including an appeal to the international community to send human rights monitors and peacekeepers inside Burma immediately, and to prosecute the SPDC for genocide and crimes against humanity. In his speech, Mr Pitts told Congress that if the US Government and the international community fails to act, "we will all be responsible for the successful genocide campaign and ethnic cleansing going on by the vicious military of the SPDC".[14]

While politicians who are willing to take the risk of going into a conflict zone, often illegally, to see first-hand the situation are rare, even rarer are young people who choose to go right into the heart of another country with the specific aim of challenging the brutal regime, undeterred by the prospect of being locked up. Such was the purpose, and the sacrifice, of James Mawdsley.

Inspired by the example of men like Major Seagrim, and supported by Lord Alton and Baroness Cox, James decided, not once but three times, to stage a protest in Burma. His aim was to look the regime in the eyes and ask them why they slaughter and oppress their people. He also wanted to see inside a prison for himself, to understand what political prisoners live through. He knew the only way to accomplish either aim was as a prisoner himself. A valuable by-product of his action was the international attention drawn to Burma's suffering.

James' story is told in full in his book *The Heart Must Break: The Fight for Democracy and Truth in Burma*. He first went to the region in 1996, and taught English to Burman refugees, members of the ABSDF, in Minthamee Camp inside Karen State. It was an opportunity to learn about the situation and to show support for the people there. "A strongly-worded resolution by the United Nations condemning the Burmese junta (as they do every year) means very little to a six-year-old in the jungle. In fact it means nothing," he explains. "But having a big white clown blundering around the camp is a sure sign to them that the outside world has not forgotten them. They can see that they are not abandoned, that they have friends from far away who care about them. Not words of sympathy but the reality of sharing life with them because they are worth it."[15] In explaining his motivation he added: "British politicians who had too much on their plate abandoned the Karen. Betrayed them. Left them to the mercy of the Burman majority and the fifty years of devastation that followed. I wanted to apologise for that. Not in words but by action."[16]

Through the ABSDF, he got to know the Karen and experienced himself some of the terror created by the Burma Army in Kawthoolei. Less than two months after arriving at Minthamee, word came that an attack was imminent and everyone had to flee. James wanted to stay behind to confront the attackers, but Ko Htay Aung, a resistance commander, told him to go. "Thank you for your time here. This is our soil, we can die for our soil, but you should not die for it."[17]

So James and the more than 200 people who lived in Minthamee left at night and slept in the forest. He recalls the reaction of a baby to the commotion of a river crossing:

He began struggling in my arms, trying to twist around. His eyes flared wide open and there was a look of fear in them. Until then I had not been worried about what was going on. But seeing the baby like that suddenly made me afraid. There was a massive and brutal force bearing down on vulnerable and defenceless groups. Terrible things were going to happen.[18]

James escaped, but wanted to go back. He was inspired by "people so brave and yet gentle, so tough and yet cheerful, so poor and so kind and so genuine" and he believed that what was required of him amounted to more than simply lobbying politicians, however important that may be. He began to plan his next trip.

With a large chain and pro-democracy letters in his bag, James travelled to Rangoon in September 1997. In a carefully thought-out mission, he chained himself to a school gate, shouted democracy slogans and handed out leaflets. Within a few minutes the police were on the scene. It took them an hour to cut through the chain. Then James was whisked off for questioning. His justification for what he had done puzzled the military intelligence:

"Why have you come to Burma?" the military intelligence Colonel asked.

"Because I love Burma, I love the people here and I hate what your regime is doing to them," James replied.

"It is not your country. Why do you interfere?" was the retort.

"It is one world," James explained. "It is my brothers and sisters that you are torturing, raping and murdering. It is absolutely my business to protest against that."[19]

The British and Australian embassies – he holds dual nationality – worked hard for his early release, and within a day he had been deported. But he had wanted more time with the regime, and to see inside a jail. So he returned in April 1998.

He asked the KNU to take him through the jungle to Moulmein, Burma's third largest city. It meant a long and dangerous trek through tough conditions. The Burma Army got word that a foreigner was with the Karen, and lay in wait for them for five days. Fortunately the Karen intercepted this news on their radio transmissions, and were able to avoid the trap.

A Karen boy on this journey, by the name of Ta Roe, stirred James' heart when he said that "the world will end soon. It is the Book of Revelation. The time has come." He had witnessed burning villages and the massacre of his people, but James wanted to reassure him. "Don't say that. It's not so bad, there is so much hope," he said. But he realised the severity of the situation. "I regretted saying that," he wrote in his diary. "Who was I to interpret the Bible to him? He could read it himself. I considered my arrogance in thinking of Christianity as a European's religion. Come to think of it, which is closer to Galilee, Lancashire or Karen State?"

James was born into a Catholic family and had a belief in God, but he was not overtly conscious of a personal faith when he first embarked on this commitment to justice and democracy. "I had read the Book of Revelation and the Gospel of John in the jungle, and I remember being impressed that the churches were always the best buildings in the villages, built out of smooth polished hardwood as opposed to bamboo," he said. He was also accompanied in the jungle by Karen soldiers and an army padre who regularly read from the Bible. But his faith came fully alive only once he was in jail.

Once he arrived in Moulmein, he walked through the market with a tape recorder playing Burmese democracy songs. He distributed leaflets calling for the release of political prisoners. Sentenced to five years in prison, he served 99 days. Towards the end of this time, James received a Bible from a guard. Having been bereft of reading materials and sitting in solitary confinement with little else to do, he read it cover to cover. He describes experiencing a "rapturous love".

Scriptures leapt out at him as if in confirmation of the purpose he had already chosen for his life. 1 John 3:17–18 was one. It says: "If anyone has material possessions and sees his brother in need but has no pity on him, how can the love of God be in him? Dear children, let us not love with words or tongue, but with actions and in truth."

Another was Micah 6:8 – "He has showed you, O man, what is good. And what does the Lord require of you? To act justly and to love mercy and to walk humbly with your God."

Hell for James turned into heaven. "It did not matter that I was in prison," he writes in his book. "I felt God's love, overwhelming, terrifying, everlasting love bubbling up within me, and overflowing . . . All of creation seemed wonderful: blades of grass, a ray of sunlight, the concrete floor of my cell."[20]

During this encounter with God, James surrendered his life to God and vowed that if the Lord wanted him to stay in prison for the rest of his life, he was willing to do it. A day later he was released.

Those 99 days were harsh. James caught scabies, suffered brutal torture and beatings, and – until he received a Bible – he felt deeply depressed. But when he was released, he felt he had not yet done enough – he still had to confront the regime. So in 1999 he returned to Burma and, once again, handed out democracy letters in the street. He went in guided by Karenni soldiers, and on the way the group bumped into some Burma Army soldiers. Four of James' companions were shot.

The Burmese junta was furious that James had defied them once again and had not been broken by his 99 days in jail the previous year. This time they lashed out and sentenced him to an unbelievable 17 years behind bars.

That sentence was perhaps the biggest mistake the junta made in James' case. If they had given him a couple of years, the international community might not have noticed. Britain and Australia would probably have made little protest, and may even have argued that James was irresponsible and deserved what he got. But no one could dismiss a 17-year sentence. An international campaign developed and pressure on the junta mounted. The United Nations Working Group on Arbitrary Detention found entirely in James' favour, the Pope wrote to the Chinese Government to ask them to use their influence with Rangoon, and Christians and other human rights activists from various organisations lobbied on James' behalf. Candlelit vigils were held and letters were signed by US Congressmen.

On 20th October, 2000, the Burmese authorities had had enough. James' case was gaining too much attention and it was exposure that they could do without. So after fourteen months of a 17-year sentence, James was released. In a letter to Christian Solidarity Worldwide, one organisation which had campaigned for his release, he wrote this:

> I would like to give my deepest thanks to CSW for your help whilst I was in Burma. You worked and prayed so effectively first of all to keep me well and then to get me out at the right time. And there is another feeling which goes beyond gratitude. Namely I rejoice at being part of the body of Christ, of sharing that Life with you.
>
> When somebody helps me, the worldly part of me gives them thanks, but the spiritual part of me gives praise to God. As I am delighted to discover and receive the good which is in the world, then as well as thanking the person who carried that good, I give thanks and praise to the source of that good, which is God.
>
> All members of CSW are aware of the terrible suffering in Burma so I do not need to explain about that. But I would like to explain about the effectiveness of your work. I have been on the receiving end of your generosity, campaigning, letters and prayers. Now I am out of prison, yet with your help, I was free throughout.
>
> However hard prison was I knew that I was still showered with more blessings than I could possibly count. I remained full of hope and a quiet joy. It was obvious to me that such blessings could not have come from my prayers alone, that rather there must be an awful lot of other people having their prayers for me answered. And as the year went by I received more and more letters and cards from CSW members which confirmed just that. Christ is in the world. Inasmuch as we are obedient to Him, then we are part of His Body. That Body then cannot be overcome, it cannot be prevailed against. And so long as I could remain faithful to Christ, who is the Head of the Body, then I had nothing to fear. The military junta in Burma is ruthless, cruel and oppressive to mankind. Yet against God it is as nothing.
>
> And so in fact all the junta's assaults and attacks rebounded upon themselves. The more they lied the stupider they looked. The worse the conditions they kept me in the stronger became the pressure upon them from abroad. And the more violently they treated

me then the greater the outrage grew. In the end the regime gave up the fight because, blind as they are, even they recognised that they could not prevail against a united force for right.

My thanks then to you because I was never alone, and because I was confident always of being on the winning side. God bless you.

There are many other foreigners – "young white brothers and sisters" – who have sacrificed much for the Karen cause. Some are missionaries, others activists, some humanitarian relief workers. Some are Christians, others are not. Some engage in the armed struggle, providing military training, procuring weapons and equipment, and planning strategy. Others speak and write on behalf of the Karens.

Saw Sarky, for example, is one "white brother" who is now considered a full Karen leader. A hotelier born in Milan of Armenian origin and now living in Portugal, he represents the KNU in Europe and is a member of the Central Committee. He is also the KNU's Special Envoy to East Timor, and the NDF's representative in Europe.

Stephanie Lee dedicated her life to the Karenni people – and, tragically, gave her life in the process. In November 2001 this young English woman, still at university, was killed in a motorcycle accident while working in the refugee camps around Mae Hong Son. When her funeral was held, 4,000 people attended, and she was buried in one of the Karenni camps. Her parents and brother have continued the work of the charity she founded, the Karenni Student Development Programme, because Stephanie's belief was that education is the key to an end to the suffering in Burma.

The Karen Action Group, Karen Aid, Partners and various other organisations, many of them Christian, have been established to serve the Karen and other ethnic nationalities in Burma. Chrestos Mission, a medical charity, states that its purpose is "bringing Christ's kindness to the Karen and Karenni people". Christians Concerned for Burma, a group involved in education, relief and evangelism and linked to the Free Burma Rangers, initiated the Global Day of Prayer for Burma. All these people are examples to us all of what is possible for a "Westerner" to do, and they all demonstrate that the people of Burma are not some alien race far away. They are our brothers and sisters. As James Mawdsley has said, "Mankind is one body. We cannot move forward except together. We cannot leave parts of our body behind. None of us is free until we all are free."[21]

NOTES

1 As quoted by Jonathan Falla, *True Love and Bartholomew: Rebels on the Burmese Border*, p. 25
2 Andrew Boyd, *Baroness Cox: A Voice for the Voiceless*
3 Ibid.
4 Ibid.
5 Ibid.
6 "Burma accused of germ warfare", *The Sunday Times*, November 20th, 1994
7 "Rangoon linked to germ warfare", *The Times*, November 15th, 1994
8 Boyd
9 Ibid.
10 Ibid.
11 *Hansard*, House of Lords, December 3rd, 2002
12 *Hansard*, House of Lords, June 24th, 2003
13 Crickett Dodge, *Partners World*, first quarter, 2003
14 Mr Pitts, H. Res 84, 1st Session, House of Representatives, 108th Congress, February 13th, 2003
15 James Mawdsley, *The Heart Must Break*
16 Ibid.

17 Ibid.
18 Ibid.
19 Ibid.
20 Ibid.
21 Ibid.

CHAPTER NINE

FAITH OR FEAR?

"These are they who have come out of the great tribulation;
They have washed their robes and made them white in the
blood of the Lamb.
Therefore, they are before the throne of God and serve him
day and night in his temple;
And he who sits on the throne will spread his tent over
them.
Never again will they hunger; never again will they thirst.
The sun will not beat upon them, nor any scorching heat.
For the Lamb at the centre of the throne will be their
shepherd;
He will lead them to springs of living water.
And God will wipe away every tear from their eyes."
Revelation 7:14–17

Eleven-year-old Kyow Zeya sat at the bus stop in Rangoon. School was over, and he was on his way to visit his aunt. But he never got there. As he sat munching a snack and nonchalantly playing with a stick, an army truck pulled up at the curb. Burma Army soldiers got out, grabbed him, and told him he had to join the army. He has not seen his family since.

"Were you given a choice?" I asked as he told his story to me from the safety of a Karen leader's home in Thailand.

"The choice was: join the army or go to jail," he replied. "I had no choice."

Composed and articulate, Kyow Zeya, a Burman Buddhist now aged fourteen, seemed mature beyond his years. But his eyes betrayed a haunted look which spoke of the fear he had lived under. His childhood innocence had been stripped away.

After his capture, he was taken to Ta Kyin Koe First Battalion Camp in Danyigorn, where at least 30 children of a similar age were being held. After eight months there, he was sent to the Byay Ma Na military training camp in the Tatmadaw's 5th Battalion area. He went through five months of basic military training, which included running five or six miles each morning. He was then dispatched to join the Light Infantry Battalion 341 in Papun district, Karen State, from where, after a few days, he was sent to the front line. In a unit of 30 soldiers, he claimed, fifteen were his age.

In eight months on the front line, Kyow Zeya witnessed numerous attacks on villages. He saw Karen villagers being rounded up and forced to work as porters for the army. Burma Army soldiers were under orders to burn, rape and kill whenever they entered a Karen village, he said. "There was no law."

Beatings were regular. Kyow Zeya was beaten several times for failing to carry a gun. He was fed anti-Karen propaganda, which included warnings from the SPDC that if he ever ran away and had the misfortune to fall into the hands of the Karen resistance, they would torture and kill him brutally. However, after eight months on the front line, he had had enough. Although he believed the propaganda, he no longer cared. "I did believe that the Karen were very bad, and I knew that if I escaped, I might face the Karen," he admitted. "But I did not want to live."

He escaped from the Tatmadaw, and was almost immediately captured by the KNLA. He felt afraid at first, but after a while he realised that the SPDC's propaganda was false. Now being sheltered by the Karen, Kyow Zeya said he feels "safe and free and loved". A total contrast to his life in the Tatmadaw which, he said, "was like hell".

Kyow Zeya is not unusual. There are estimated to be 70,000 child soldiers in the Tatmadaw, making up 20 per cent of the total number of troops. The process for recruiting child soldiers follows a consistent pattern – grabbing kids off the street from bus stops and on their way home from school.

Fourteen-year-old Yang suffered a similar fate to Kyow Zeya. At 9 p.m. on 30th August, 2002, he was on his way home after an evening tutorial class in Insein, just outside Rangoon. It was dark. He walked quickly, whistling quietly to himself. He was tired, but content. Then suddenly from out of the shadows came a policeman and a soldier. They grabbed him and told him he was to join the Burma Army.

That same night, just three hours earlier in Daongwa, at least one other boy was taken. Sixteen-year-old Nay strolled home from his after-school class at 6 p.m. A car drew up alongside him as he walked, and three soldiers got out. "I was told I was being taken to serve as a soldier. I was told to keep quiet and not ask questions. When I said I did not want to be a soldier, they told me to shut up. They said I had a choice: if I did not join the army, I would go to jail."

Yang and Nay, like Kyow Zeya before them, were taken to a military recruiting centre in Mingladaw and held there for several days. Then they underwent military training. They saw many other child soldiers at Mingladaw. Yang claimed that out of 1,750 new recruits, at least 1,000 were children under 16. Fourteen-year-old Chit, another forced conscript, said that at Yamadin training base where he had been taken, 100 out of 250 new soldiers were children.

Pay was poor and beatings were commonplace. Yang was paid 4,500 kyats a month – but a basket of rice, he points out, costs 10,000 kyats. Nay was beaten so badly that he could not walk for a week. The reason for such savage punishment? "I had tripped over a small box," he said. Chit was beaten on one occasion by nine men, because he had been late for a line-up. Yang said the child soldiers were beaten regularly with sticks, and if one person made a mistake, the whole section was beaten.

Yang and Nay never engaged in combat, but they worked on the front line as guards, assisting military intelligence with communications, and collecting firewood. But they saw many other children forced to fight.

After just three weeks in Battalion 343, Nay decided to run away. He had completed four months' military training but, he said, "I could not bear the torture anymore." He hatched an escape plan and shared the idea with Yang. The younger boy agreed to go too, and one day they told their superiors that they were going out to collect firewood. As soon as they were out of sight, they ran down the mountain and straight into the arms of the KNLA.

Yang and Nay had also been warned by the SPDC about the brutality of the Karen but, unlike Kyow Zeya, they did not believe it. They were not afraid when the KNLA caught them and, they said, since then the Karen have looked after them very well. Yang, a young-looking fourteen-year-old, was taken immediately to a safe-house in Thailand. Nay, because he looks older, was kept as a prisoner in a cell in a KNLA base for a few days and interrogated, but he said he was never tortured and was well treated. He too was then taken to a place of safety.

These boys are the lucky ones. "Now I can try to find my future," said Yang. "If I had stayed in the army, my future would be hopeless." Nay agreed. "If I had stayed in the army, I could have got malaria, or been shot by the KNLA, and I could have died." Now enjoying his freedom, he urges other child soldiers in the Tatmadaw to defect. "They should flee, and be free to study." But that is easier said than done, and the consequences if they are caught in the process of escaping are immense.

Kyow Zeya looked me in the eye as he finished telling his story. I asked him if he had a request, a message to take out to the world. "It is not good for a child to be a soldier. Tell the international community to speak to the regime," he said. "Tell them not to grab children and force them to be soldiers." Nay had exactly the same message. "Please tell the world to put pressure on the SPDC to stop using child soldiers."

The KNLA and other resistance armies in Burma have child soldiers too, but there is a huge difference. In the Burma Army, children do not volunteer – they are forced. In the KNLA, children are discouraged from joining but, if they choose to do so, they are accepted. While this still may not make it right, it is a distinguishing feature between the two sides. Karen boys who join the KNLA usually do so having seen their own parents slaughtered before their eyes. They have no stomach for schooling, even though their elders try to persuade them to go to school – they want to fight the people who killed their parents. That was the case, for example, for thirteen-year-old Pokolah, who saw his parents and relatives tortured and killed, and his village burned down. Fifteen-year-old Sayramon experienced exactly the same.[1]

For the Shan, the situation is similar. Colonel Yawd Serk, leader of the Shan State Army (SSA) and the Restoration Council of the Shan States (RCSS), explained that the only children in the ranks of the SSA are ones who have been found wandering in the jungle, orphaned and displaced. When SSA soldiers find such children, they take them to centres of internally displaced people near the Thai border. But on the way, according to the Colonel, they "share their uniforms and guns with the children" so that they have some clothes to wear and can defend themselves in the event of an attack. As soon as they are taken to a safe area, they are sent to school. Apart from this being the right and compassionate thing to do, it also makes military sense. "Young children with not enough experience are useless in battle," said Colonel Yawd Serk. "They are risking their lives and the lives of their comrades."

The catalogue of terror carried out by the SPDC must surely provoke questions in our minds about how such depravity can take place. What is it that causes a regime, even one that is intolerant of democracy and dissent, to behave so brutally? How is it that Tatmadaw soldiers can find the will to tie eight-year-old children to a tree and use them as target practice, or put a baby in a rice pounder and crush it to death? What threat do those children, or that baby, pose to them? How is it that soldiers do not stop at their ordinary military duty – shooting – which in itself is bad but is what all armies do? But instead, they denigrate their opponents in the most barbaric ways. Go Nai, for example, was attacked at 8 p.m. on 11th September, 1994 when Burma Army troops entered his village. They cut his nose off, gouged his eyes out, stabbed his ears while he was still alive, and then finished him off with a knife to his chest.[2] Why?

It is difficult if not impossible to truly understand, and therefore to answer the question "why?" One can put it down to the old adage that "power corrupts and absolute power corrupts absolutely", but Daw Aung San Suu Kyi believes that is not quite true. "It is not power that corrupts but fear," she said. "Fear of losing power corrupts those who wield it and fear of the scourge of power corrupts those who are subject to it."[3] That, on a political level, goes some way to answering the question "why?" On a theological and moral level, one could argue that it is all related to the fall of man, to basic human sin. Sin, it is said, passes through each and every human heart and the question is how we respond to that sin. In Romans we are taught that we have all sinned and fallen short of the glory of God. The answer, as it says in Romans 6:12, is "Do not let sin reign in your mortal body so that you obey its evil desires." But there is something more to the Burmese junta's depravity than just basic human sin, and it is hard to pinpoint. There is something demonic. The SPDC is a stronghold of evil.

But it does not profit us or benefit those who are suffering if we spend all our time analysing and deliberating over why the SPDC behaves in this way. Of more value is to ask ourselves some questions about our own society. How is it that when we have such bountiful freedom – freedom to worship, to choose our government, to express our opinions without fear of being imprisoned, to move and associate wherever and with whoever we choose – we indulge ourselves in those freedoms and fail to use them for others? How is it that the free world has not made more noise about the evils perpetrated in Burma? Martin Luther King once said that "the greatest sin of our time is not the few who have destroyed, but the many who have remained silent". While there are foreigners who have used their freedom to work for the freedom of Burma, and some of them have been mentioned in this book, there are many people who are still ignorant or apathetic about Burma. Why do we allow the suffering in Burma to continue?

It is partly a matter of government policy. The United States has taken the strongest lead but other countries have not followed. While the US introduced a total ban on new investment in Burma in 1996, and the Burma Freedom and Democracy Act in 2003 which imposed severe economic sanctions, the European Union (EU) and the Association of South East Asian Nations (ASEAN) have dragged their feet. While US Secretary of State Colin Powell wrote in an article in the *Wall Street Journal* in 2003 describing the SPDC, accurately, as "thugs", ASEAN and Australia still talk in terms of "engagement". The EU has adopted a Common Position which includes an arms embargo, a ban on visas for SPDC officials, suspension of defence links and non-humanitarian aid, and a ban on high-level official visits, but it could do more. Similarly, ASEAN for the first time ever criticised the re-arrest of Daw Aung San Suu Kyi in 2003, but Burma remains a member of ASEAN and ASEAN's policy of non-interference in the internal affairs of other countries binds its hands. But Colonel Nerdah Mya asks the question: "How can genocide, the killing of innocent civilians, rape, looting, destruction and involvement in the drugs trade be an 'internal matter'? It is an international matter."

But we should not be looking only to governments for help. In Proverbs 31:8–9 it says: "Speak up for those who cannot speak for themselves, for the rights of all who are destitute. Speak up and judge fairly; defend the rights of the poor and needy." That does not apply only to politicians. God calls all of us to do that. In Micah 6:8, it does not say "He has showed you, O United Nations, ASEAN, EU and national governments" – it says "He has showed you, O *man*, what is good. And what does the Lord require of you? To act justly and to love mercy and to walk humbly with your God." We therefore have a duty to act. Daw Aung San Suu Kyi once said that "sometimes it is better to have the people of the world on your side than the governments of the world", and her father, General Aung San, has good words for us in this context: "Don't just depend on the courage and intrepidity of others. Each and every one of you must make sacrifices to become a hero possessed of courage and intrepidity. Then only shall we all be able to enjoy true freedom."[4] We do not all need to be heroes, but we do all need to contribute to the search for true freedom.

Something else is wrong too. How is it that in our society, where we have plenty, we get angry at the slightest mishap? Perhaps I should not generalise, but I speak for myself. I get annoyed if there is a traffic jam and I am running late, I get impatient in a supermarket queue, I get upset if my computer crashes. Yet in contrast to my comfortable life, the Karen – who live in a place of fear and terror and often do not know where the next meal will come from or how they will treat their sick – have the grace to smile, to laugh, to give so generously, and to sing with such joy songs like "Stand up, stand up for Jesus, ye soldiers of the Cross" and "I'm so glad that Jesus set me free!" Westerners think that we can give to the Karen, and in some ways we can and should, but we should do so remembering that the Karen have much, spiritually, to teach us.

On 20th May, 2002 I had the privilege of attending the celebration of freedom and independence in a land not dissimilar to Kawthoolei. East Timor had been a Portuguese colony, until 1975 when the Portuguese withdrew suddenly. Before the East Timorese had a chance to express their desire, Indonesia launched a brutal invasion. During the 24-year occupation, over 200,000 people, up to a quarter of the population, died, either directly at the hands of the Indonesian military or through famine and disease caused by the occupation. Until the fall of Suharto, the situation seemed hopeless. Then, very suddenly, the situation in Indonesia changed, Suharto was toppled, and Indonesia agreed to allow the United Nations to organise a referendum to determine the future of East Timor. Even then, the Indonesian military – from whom the SPDC learned many of their tactics – sought to divide the Timorese by creating militia gangs to terrorise their own people. In a strategy remarkably similar to the creation of the DKBA among the Karen, the militia were armed, paid, controlled and directed by the Indonesian military. Like the DKBA, they were reportedly given drugs to spur them on in their crazed acts of violence. They wrought terror and chaos in East Timor. But despite the intimidation, the referendum went ahead, and the people voted overwhelmingly for independence. The Indonesian military and their militia responded to the result by unleashing a wave of violence, burning down 80 per cent of the capital, Dili, and causing the displacement of 200,000 people. However, the international community finally stepped in, Indonesia withdrew, and the world's newest nation was born.

As I stood there in Dili on 20th May and sang the national anthem, I turned to the man next to me, a friend who I had known for several years. He had been the first Timorese to be exiled from his country, in 1975. His name was Father Fransisco Fernandes. It was midnight, and the flag was being raised for the first time. I asked him whether he had believed that he would ever live to see this day when his country was free.

"Yes I did," he said with a gentle smile. "Throughout our struggle, people all around the world said to me 'why do you bother? You are fighting a losing battle. Indonesia will never give your people freedom, the world will never help you, so why do you carry on?' But we had one thing those people did not know about. We trusted God. This was a victory of faith."

I am confident that the Karen people, and all those engaged in the fight for democracy and truth in Burma, possess the same faith, courage, determination, persistence and trust in God that the East Timorese resistance had. I trust that one day they will achieve their goal.

In 1989 the East Timorese Nobel Laureate, Bishop Carlos Belo, wrote a letter to the United Nations Secretary-General in which he called for international assistance and uttered the chilling words: "We are dying as a people and a nation." It was ten years before the UN responded. In 1992, General Bo Mya wrote a similar letter to the UN Secretary-General, in which he said that "The struggle of the Karen people is simply to restore the land of our forefathers; it is a struggle for the survival of the Karen people." The letter was written a month after ten Burmese aeroplanes, supplied by China, had bombed the hills around Manerplaw. "We call upon you to use your good offices to prevent the further loss of human life amongst innocent villagers," Bo Mya pleaded with the Secretary-General. "Only the Security Council has the power to prevent the current full-scale war from escalating even further, and to save a distinct ethnic population from the threat of annihilation." Maybe one day the UN will answer Bo Mya's letter.

Winston Churchill, at the start of the Second World War, had this to say, and his words are appropriate today: "You ask, what is our policy? I will say: It is to wage war, by sea, land and air, with all our might and with all the strength that God can give us; to wage war against a monstrous tyranny, never surpassed in the dark, lamentable catalogue of human crime. That is our policy. You ask what is our aim? I can answer in one word: victory, victory at all costs, victory however long and hard the road may be."

Some of the Karen are waging this war militarily, not by sea or air but on the land, and they deserve our prayers. Some are fighting politically, through diplomatic efforts in the political forums of the world. But all of us, in whatever other trenches, military or political, we may be called to fight in, can be engaged in this war spiritually. What we cannot afford to do is be apathetic. Each one of us can do something. We can pray, write letters, give money, medicine, school books, or visit the refugees. As Sally Panter wrote in her diary in Manerplaw, "never say the Lord cannot use you. For everyone is needed and if we refuse it may be that something will not be done, that some tasks will go undone."

If people in the free world choose, practically and spiritually, to stand with the Karen, the rewards are great. Evil cannot prosper. In the Karen Refugee Committee's report after the death of Ne Win in 2002, it said: "Ne Win died friendless and disgraced. No one came out with a good word for him.

Even his friends and accomplices kept their distance. Now he belongs to history, in the company of Hitler, Eichman, Tojo, Mobutu and Pol Pot." And although Ne Win's key lieutenants are still in charge, the report claimed, there is "much room for optimism". In contrast to Ne Win, the Karen do have friends. "There are people who are ready to risk life and limb, to speak out for freedom, for harmony and equality. There are those who are ready to stand up for righteousness and justice. There are people ready to share what they have. To these people, we have only appreciation and gratitude."

Pastor Simon's words echo these thoughts. In a letter to me on 20th August, 2002, he wrote:

> The works of dedicated and committed people like you, James Mawdsley, David Alton, Dr Martin Panter, Caroline Cox and many others brought tremendous hope and encouragement to us who are suffering and going through all kinds of atrocities . . . We want to go home. We want peace to be restored to our country so that we can go back. But though things around seem very dark and dim, we are strongly convinced that the Lord is in control of all and He will intervene and change the situation in Burma . . . It is His word that keeps us focusing our eyes on the Lord Jesus Christ and giving us hope to struggle and try the best we can to serve Him through serving His sons and daughters.

He ended his letter with this challenge:

"Please pray, work hard and be prepared to help when the time comes for our repatriation. Our God is able, and He will intervene and reveal His mighty power for His glory and honour."

NOTES

1 CSW Report, Visit to the Thai–Burmese border, December 7th–13th, 1996

2 CSW Report, Visit to the Thai–Burmese border, November 3rd–10th, 1994

3 Aung San Suu Kyi, Essay to commemorate the European Parliament's award of the 1990 Sakharov Prize for Freedom of Thought, published in *The Times Literary Supplement, The New York Times, The Far Eastern Economic Review, The Bangkok Post, The Times of India* and other publications

4 Aung San, quoted in Aung San Suu Kyi's Essay

BIBLIOGRAPHY

Boyd, Andrew, *Baroness Cox: A Voice for the Voiceless*, Lion, 1998

Christian Solidarity Worldwide, Reports on Visits to the Thai–Burmese Border: 1994, 1995, 1996, 1997, 1998, 1999, 2000, 2001, 2002, 2003

Falla, Jonathan, *True Love And Bartholomew: Rebels on the Burmese Border*, Cambridge University Press, 1991

Fink, Christina, *Living Silence: Burma Under Military Rule*, Zed Books, 2001

Goodden, Christian, *Three Pagodas: A Journey Down the Thai–Burmese Border*, Second Revised & Expanded Edition, Jungle Books, 2002

House of Lords debates, *Hansard Official Report*, 15 May 1997, 25 March 1998, 3 December 2002, 24 June 2003

Human Rights Watch, *"My Gun Was As Tall As Me" – Child Soldiers in Burma*, 2002

Khoo Thwe, Pascal, *From the Land of Green Ghosts*, Harper-Collins, 2002

Lintner, Bertil, *Burma in Revolt: Opium and Insurgency since 1948*, Silkworm Books, 1994

Marshall, Harry Ignatius, *The Karen People of Burma: A*

Study in Anthropology and Ethnology, White Lotus Press, 1997 (first published 1922)

Mawdsley, James, *The Heart Must Break: The Fight for Democracy and Truth in Burma*, Random House, 2001

Mirante, Edith, *Burmese Looking Glass: A Human Rights Adventure and A Jungle Revolution*, Atlantic Monthly Press, 1993

Moo Troo, Saw, *Karens and Communism*

Morrison, Ian, *Grandfather Longlegs: The Life and Gallant Death of Major H.P. Seagrim*, Faber & Faber, 1946

Po, San C, *Burma and the Karens*, White Lotus Press, 2001 (first published 1928)

Refugees International, *No Safe Place: Burma's Army and the Rape of Ethnic Women*, 2003

Richardson, Don, *Eternity in their Hearts*, Regal Books, 1981

Rollings, Micah, (Mika Rolley), *Karens' Fight for Peace*

Sargent, Inge, *Twilight over Burma: My Life as a Shan Princess*, University of Hawaii Press, 1994

Slim, Field Marshal Viscount, *Defeat into Victory: Battling Japan in Burma and India 1942–1945*, Cooper Square Press, 2000

Smeaton, Donald Mackenzie, *The Loyal Karens of Burma*, Kegan Paul Trench & Co, 1887

Smith, Martin, *Burma: Insurgency and the Politics of Ethnicity*, Second (updated) edition, Zed Books, 1999

Tucker, Shelby, *Among the Insurgents: Walking Through Burma*, Flamingo, 2001

Tucker, Shelby, *Burma: The Curse of Independence*, Pluto Press, 2001

US Congress, House of Representatives, 10th Congress, H. Res 84, February 13, 2003

Victor, Barbara, *The Lady: Burma's Aung San Suu Kyi*, Silkworm, 1998

Weller, John, *The Karens' Long Struggle*, Focus, November/December 1981

Christian Solidarity Worldwide (CSW) is a human rights charity working for religious freedom and justice around the world, with a particular focus on the persecuted church. Please contact CSW at the following addresses for further information:

CSW UK
PO Box 99
New Malden
Surrey KT3 3YF
United Kingdom
Tel: 0208 942 8810
http://www.csw.org.uk

CSW USA
http://www.cswusa.com

CSW Australia
Tel/Fax: (61) 75445 5787
Email: cswoz@hotmail.com

CSW Hong Kong
Tel/Fax: (852) 2591 5403
Email: admin@csw.org.hk
http://www.csw.org.hk

For information about the Global Day of Prayer for Burma, see www.prayforburma.org